"HEY, TEACH!"

Annemarieke (Mieke) Tazelaar

ISBN:172278606X
ISBN 13: 978-1722786069

Other Books by Annemarieke Tazelaar

Apple Eater

A novel based on my family's
experiences in the The Netherlands
during World War II

The Crayon Box

A collection of short stories
inspired by the names of crayons,
within the framework of a longer story

Lavender

A novella about a five-year span
of a teenage girl, who has to make
a difficult choice about her future

A Cloud of Birds

A story for young adults about the demise
of the Passenger Pigeon

Geezer Crossing

A collection of stories, both fiction and
Non-fiction, about the process of aging, and
Personalities of people in advanced years

WESTWARD - HOW?

While standing on the platform of the Chicago Union Station, I took a deep breath and boarded the *Empire Builder* to begin the journey of my dreams. I hoisted my suitcase up into the overhead compartment, then sank into my assigned seat, placing my pillow and small bag next to me. Somewhere on another car, everything else I owned in the world was packed in two trunks. I felt a small jerk as the train began its trek across the Midwest states to the West Coast. Shivering with excitement, I snuggled into the space that was solely mine for the next two-and-a-half half days.

Thirteen years earlier, in 1946, right after World War II, my family had come to the United States from the Netherlands and settled in Grand Rapids, Michigan. The next year, when I was ten, I wrote to the Chamber of Commerce of every capital city in my new homeland and asked them for information about their state. I received back a generous assortment of brochures, post cards, and books with photographs, all free.

After weeks poring over information, my dream of living in Oregon began. In my mind I fashioned a village that lay by the Pacific Ocean. Our house, picket fence et al, which I would share with my husband and two sets of twins, had a view of the beach and was shaded by firs and cedars. Behind the house loomed tall, snow-peaked mountains. Our lives would be impossibly happy.

I packed away those dreams in lieu of the reality of school, jobs, and getting a teaching degree. By the time I had finished a semester of my senior year at the University of Michigan, I had barely thought of where I would teach. Grand Rapids? I was sure I could get a job there.

In the Fifties, school districts all over the country sent recruiters to talk to graduating "Education" majors. I made appointments with representatives from Chicago, Detroit, Flint, and Milwaukee, all logical choices. But then I noticed on the list, Long Beach, California, and I thought, why not? It's the West. Was that vivid, naïve dream of my childhood possible? I had a long conversation with a woman from Long Beach, and she as much as hired me. "My dear, I'm not authorized to make a final decision, but if you want to start packing your bags"… but I wasn't ready to make up my mind.

Though no recruiter had come from Portland, Seattle, or any other Northwest city, I soon decided that this is where I really wanted to be. Comparing salaries, I narrowed my choice to three smaller cities in Washington, then wrote to the school districts in Olympia, Bremerton, and Bellingham, stating that I wanted to teach junior high school.

Each sent back application forms, but Bremerton requested a letter, as well. They wanted me to answer three questions: Why did I want to teach? Why, of all age groups, was I choosing junior high? And why did I want to come to the Northwest?

Women entering colleges and universities in the Fifties had two or three fields open to them. One was nursing. I explained that I was not a fan of exposed blood, mine or anybody else's, so nursing was out of the question. But my experience as a student teacher in junior high showed me that junior high kids had dropped out of the human race, and I felt it my mission to help them find their way back. In spite of their alien behavior, they seemed to like me and gave me a marginal, but acceptable amount of respect, though most of them were just nine years younger than I at that time.

It was what I wrote about mountains, I later learned, that earned me a modicum of fame in the Bremerton School District. I explained that I had never seen a mountain in my life. I wrote that the highest point in my native the Netherlands was a few hundred feet above sea level.

I knew that Michigan had a bump in its topography, all of five hundred feet high, that residents dared to call a mountain. I understood that real mountains were often covered with snow, and that they probably looked different from white clouds on the horizon. I surmised that mountains were three-dimensional and wanted to know what it felt like to be surrounded by them.

The letter traveled around the district, apparently, and in 1959, just before Spring Break, I received a phone call in my dorm from Mr. Jarstad, the Bremerton Superintendent of Schools. He asked if I could come for an interview. I told him that this was, unfortunately, impossible, because I had no money.

"I like your voice," he told me. "If you want the job, it's yours."

"You mean I'm hired? Just like that?" I asked.

"You are. Just like that. We need someone at Coontz Junior High to teach English and social studies. Will that suit you?"

"Of course!" I said, hoping my enthusiastic squeak masked my terror.

Of course? I truly had no money. My parents had no idea that I had even applied this far away from home.

My stomach, which had never been happy with sudden emotional upheavals, lurched. I bolted for the bathroom.

I went home a few days later. "I have a teaching job for next year," I announced during dinner, in a sort of ho-hum fashion.

My father smiled at me. "Congratulations! Where? Grand Rapids?"

I stared at him and at my mother. "Not Grand Rapids."

Mother put her hand over her open mouth, then said, "Oregon!"

"Bremerton, Washington."

"Where is that?" they chimed in unison. On another planet. Somewhere between Jupiter and Saturn.

Mother voiced her dismay, even cried a bit. That was her job. But this was an irreversible decision, and she knew it. From then on, I had their support. They could not help me financially, so that summer, I worked several jobs and scraped together $250 for a train ticket, hotel for two nights in Seattle, a ferry ride, one month's rent, and enough for food and other essentials to tide me over until I received my first pay check in October.

And here I was on this brilliant day in early September, on my way to fulfill my dream. The *Empire Builder* sped west across Wisconsin. I climbed to the observation deck and gazed at the grandeur of the Mississippi River, while eating a sandwich Mother had packed for me. By this time, I had become acquainted with others in my car. Ronald, an Englishman traveling to Seattle and then down the West Coast, kept shaking his head, saying, "It's so big! So vast! Unbelievable."

From time to time, I entertained two small boys while their mother escaped to the bathroom or naps in her compartment. I dredged up songs and games from my babysitting days, and the three of us had a gleeful, noisy time. Our fellow travelers who scowled at us were, no doubt, Midwesterners, taking short, fearful tours of the Wild West. Those who smiled were, naturally, Westerners going home. My soulfolk. Future neighbors.

Toward nightfall, I stretched out as best I could across two seats and settled in, thankful for the pillow my mother had insisted I take along.

The next day, we traveled across North Dakota, where miles of wheat fields continued, hour after hour. After a while, tired of the "endless waves of grain," I pulled a book out of my purse - Ayn Rand's *Atlas Shrugged*. A week ago, I had found it, washed up on a Lake Michigan beach, waterlogged and with half the cover torn off. Also missing was a chunk of pages, including the first part of Chapter One. Starting on page 13, I muddled through the next fifty pages until I got the gist of the story. I tried to sympathize with Dagney Taggard, traveling across the United States on her father's Reardon Railroad, brooding about the "Shallowness of Society."

We entered Montana, and the terrain became slightly more diversified. I closed the book and, shoving Dagney and her angst deep into my purse, I stared out of the window with renewed anticipation.

Sometime in the early afternoon, I saw my first mountains. Tiny dark shapes appeared on the horizon, so slight, hardly anything more than a defining line, but different from the blue sky meeting flat land, which I had been seeing for over a day. An hour later, I could discern more than mere silhouettes. The hills displayed contours, valleys, and shadows. Evening approached. Still, I stayed upstairs, drinking in every detail until we entered the pass. No moon shone on the elusive landscape, and soon, I could see nothing but my reflection in the dark window.

I went back to my seat, grateful that the space next to me was still unoccupied, and created a nest for the night. My pillow cushioned my head against the side of the train while I pretzeled my legs across the extra seat.

The rhythm of the wheels over the rail seams, now so much part of my journey, lulled me into sleepiness, and I knew my fantasy was becoming real. I could no longer see anything, but I knew I was in the midst of Rockies.

When dawn turned to daylight the next morning, the train was well on the western side of Washington's Stevens Pass. Cedars and firs blanketed the steep hills of the Cascades on either side of the train, and I felt, not only encircled by my fantasized mountains, but wrapped into their folds. Nothing I had ever experienced in my life came close to this sensation.

I knew one person in Seattle, and when I arrived at the King Street Station, Mia and her friend Al were there to greet me. We arranged to have my trunks transported to the State Ferry docks, then we toured the downtown area of the city.

Mia worked in the Norton Building, at that time one of the tallest in Seattle. We rode the elevator to the top floor and climbed steep stairs to the roof.

All day, I had watched Mount Rainier with amazement, as it seemed to move from one part of the skyline to another. Between buildings. Peeking over a hill. Popping up at the end of a street. Criss-crossed by telephone wires.

Now my view was unobstructed. The day was glorious, the sky, a dazzling blue: not a cloud, only my tears blurred the overwhelming vision of this god of mountains.

Beyond Rainier, I saw the snowy peaks of Adams and St. Helens. To the west, the rugged skyline of the Olympics was etched in pink. Mia pointed to Mount Baker in the north. To the east rose the Cascades I had crossed by train. I was surrounded by mountains, my impossible dream realized. Looking down at Elliott Bay, I saw a green and white ferry churning through the sparkling water. Tomorrow, it would carry me across Puget Sound to my new life.

I was home.

CAREER LAUNCH IN BREMERTON

I explored the downtown area on my own the next day: Pike Street Market, Ye Olde Curiosity Shop, Ivar's on the Waterfront, and watched greedy squawking sea gulls dive for tasty morsels in the murky water. The following day, I arranged to have my trunks loaded onto the ferry to Bremerton and walked aboard on my very first boat trip over Elliott Bay and Puget Sound.

I was met by two teachers from my school, who drove me to a cedar-paneled studio apartment above a one-car garage. The tiny, fragrant studio contained all that I needed: a hide-a-bed couch, a few other pieces of furniture, towels and bedding, and a fully-equipped kitchen. It would become my home for the next few years.

That evening, I unpacked all my wordly belongings and stashed the empty trunks in a storage space.

I had a few days to myself before going to my first meeting, so I walked around town and marveled at the riot of colors I saw in yards: so many diverse flowers and crysanthamums the size of dinner plates!

A few days later, I attended a district-wide orientation and soon after, walked into my new teaching career at Coontz Junior High. I was the only faculty member under forty years of age, and I felt intimidated. Was I really allowed to call these colleagues by their first names? But they were helpful and kind.

Florence, a veteran teacher, told me, "Now, if you have any problems with the students, just come and get me. I'm right across the hall, and I will be right over. I'm bigger and meaner than you are, and they will listen to me!"

I thanked her, knowing that I would never resort to that. By the time I welcomed my first class, the stomach butterflies, which had been fluttering for the past four months, all but disappeared.

Those little buggers returned an hour into my first class, when I realized that the lesson plans I had made for the three sessions I was to teach the morning group, had already been exhausted. I had to improvise the rest of the time, but we were all a bit awed, my students and I. It was their first school experience since leaving their comfortable elementary school. I asked them how it felt to be in this new venture, and many voices piped up at the same time, until I set a rule about raising hands and taking turns to speak. The greatest confusion for nearly everybody was learning how to use their lockers. Since I was also their home room teacher, I felt justified in delving into this problem with them. After all, it hadn't been that many years ago since I had used lockers, and I told them I would bring a lock the next day, so we would go over the formula for opening the little devices. They were responsible for memorizing their three numbers.

By the time we got through discussing the lunch room, the five-minute challenges of getting to a class or the gym at the opposite end of the school, and the uppity eighth graders who treated them with disdain, I had successfully endured my first morning.

Before I ever greeted my very first 7th grade class, I had idealized notions of how I was going to make geniuses of all

8

my students. I loved doing research, and so naturally, I figured my students would, too.

One of the first assignments I gave them was to hand out obscure topics to delve into and explore. It did not take long for the complaints to emerge from the students, from parents, from Kathie, the "li-BAR-ien" from Texas, from the principal. What was I trying to do? How were the students supposed to find three different sources for a paper on a certain marsupial in Madagascar?

Our little library could not accommodate this information, except in the World Book Encyclopedia. The Bremerton library was a bit better, but nothing like the Grand Rapids Public Library and the University of Michigan Library, two resources I took for granted.

I quickly learned to tone down my expectations. Teachers of English and social studies during that era will attest, we had to be experts on ferreting out word-for-word plagiarism from encyclopedias.

The school counselor did not fit her role. Being sent to the principal was a bit scary for a child, but being sent to Rachel was worse. I'm not sure if she understood her job, but often, when I was in the faculty lounge, I would hear Rachel discuss a student who might have come to her in confidence, but who would certainly never return, once he or she realized how that confidence had been betrayed, passed on to the parent and to other teachers, as well.

Rachel was proud of her girls' drill team. Our school competed every spring with other schools around the area, and her group of seventh and eighth graders often won. She felt that she would have more success with just eighth graders, so she invited me to coach a seventh grade group. I thought this would be fun, and parents were delighted, as well. We practiced, as did Rachel's team, during lunch hours, marching around the city block where the school was located, so we were in full view of neighbors and drivers. We were accompanied by the school band.

Rachel watched my team one day, then commented to me, "Why not ask that fat girl to resign? She is going to spoil your chances of winning."

"You mean Sharon?" I asked. "She's really good, and she is so happy all the time. I love her energy."

"Well, then, at least, hide her in the middle of a row somewhere, where she won't be so visible."

She advised me in other ways as well. "You need to discipline those girls more. It doesn't hurt once in a while to shame someone for being out of step."

I had to admit to myself that her team personified perfection. The discipline was close to military. I wasn't especially bent on winning, just on giving the kids an enjoyable time and teaching them to cooperate. After all, I had no experience doing something like this, and their marching style did not matter that much to me, as long as they were not doing the goose step!

Nevertheless, I took it seriously, and so did my girls. They shaped up with a creative routine that we were all proud of. Several mothers made imaginative, well-designed costumes.

By the day of the competition, we knew we were ready. A number of teams marched by, and Rachel's was impressive. Her students looked straight ahead, ignoring applause from their parents. When mine appeared, I prayed they would not wave. I had forgotten to warn them about that. To my relief, they did not, but they did smile broadly when they heard their names being called. Sharon, prominently on the outside of a row where everyone could see her, was the personification of joy.

Rachel's team came in fourth. Ours, second. I had a lot to learn about diplomacy in working with Rachel on anything after that day. She was sore at me for weeks.

I was sore, too, but in a different way. I had fallen during one rehearsal and scraped one knee into a bloody mess. At the next faculty meeting, the fatherly principal, Berger Jacobson, presented me with a purple heart, smiling broadly at the amused laughter of my colleagues.

I had a good, stable initiation at Coontz, with a grandfatherly principal who seemed just as ancient to me as he did to my students. I had teacher mentors, as well as people who I would never want to emulate.

It is hard to engender fear into the hearts of eighth graders, but Miss Crawford did, as I learned later. Her bulletin board was covered with faded maxims on yellowed construction paper: *A stitch in time saves nine. The road to Hell is paved with good intentions. Look before you leap,* and other such inspirational stuff. She told me proudly that she had been in that same classroom for twenty-five years, and that she was an expert in teaching spelling and diagramming. The longer she droned on, the more my mouth went dry with dread. I knew that this would never be my fate.

Several faculty members became my role models. Florence's method of teaching was through strict discipline. "No smiling until Thanksgiving," she explained to me. Her very size awed her students. They entered her classroom meekly those first weeks, and obeyed her every command. She was fair, and she rewarded good behavior and work. Her students learned the study habits she taught them from the very first day. But by the end of November, she smiled and laughed, and her classroom, now more relaxed, exuded an atmosphere of learning through discussion and small groups of students working on projects together. She truly loved her students, and they knew it.

Agnes' classroom was homey and hospitable from the moment her students entered. Here was "grandma," and she was going to take care of them. If someone misbehaved, she tutored that child, believing that children with problems were behind in their learning skills. Many times, she did not go home until 5:30, and as that student was leaving, he or she could take a cookie out of the cookie jar, which she pulled from its hiding place beneath her desk.

I learned a lot from these two women, who became mentors and life-long friends.

Several students from those first three years made a lasting impression on me. Had I met them later, I might not have remembered them so well. One was a boy who broke my heart, because I could see his potential, but he refused to do his homework. I confronted him about that, but I did not reveal my intuition to him that he could do better. He told me that he had been told all his life how smart he was, and had decided that he just didn't have to do the work. It was a waste of his time.

"I have no way of knowing that," I told him. "I have a hunch that you are the most immature, ignorant student in this class, and you're afraid to expose that fact."

He walked out in a huff. The next day, he slammed his homework on my desk and said, "There. I did it."

It was sloppy work, and I gave him a *C-*.

He was rude and angry. "You could at least give me a *B* for turning it in."

"I grade on quality," I told him. "Not simply on getting something down on paper."

The next day he came in with a paper that was truly well done, and I graded him with a *B+*, with specific comments about what I liked. From that time on, he participated in class and turned in his work. His attitude went from cocky to being proud of being a good student. His other teachers noticed it, too. His parents thanked me. I wonder in today's climate of parents often protecting their children against their teachers, if I could have gotten away with the comment about his ignorance.

Tom, a student in my third year, was exceptional. Inspired by his hunger for knowledge, I remembered my much too ambitious endeavor of my first year, but now I took his class to the public library and taught them about research using the much larger card catalog than was available in the school library. I encouraged the students to find cross-references and be detectives about obscure bits of information. It was beyond most of the class, but Tom devoured the idea. He started going to the library on his own.

His humor set him apart from his classmates. Movies came to the school, and we were urged to show them to our classes in the movie room. Some of the films were inane, the stories being masked by dramatic music. I remember the time we watched a so-called ancient scene in Rome's Colosseum. Lions roared out of one exit onto the arena, while prisoners burst out of another door. Badly-staged fighting ensued, when Tom cried out, "Look at that poor lion over there. He doesn't have a Christian!" I nearly choked on a chuckle.

I had been concerned about him when he first joined the class late in October. His family had just moved from Wisconsin. I saw how bright he was, and his stories and essays were full of clever phrases. Yet, he seemed to be a loner, not talking to other classmates when he came in, but just sitting down and reading a book. I noticed the kids liked him and would talk to him, and he was always friendly, but non-committal.

During our first parent-teacher conference, I mentioned this to his mother. She said she had been rather concerned, too, and had talked about it with Tom.

His answer? "You know how it is, Mom. When you move to a new place, the kids that want to hang out with you right away, are not necessarily the people you want as best friends. So I'm not in a hurry."

I observed, as the year progressed, that a circle of friends developed, both boys and girls, who became positive influence on the entire class.

His mother kept in touch when I moved away, and I learned that his class was the brightest, most mature group that had ever graduated from West High. Many teachers credited this to Tom, who, they said, could see potential in an average student and make a straight A scholar out of that person.

I had a good solid beginning for the first three years of my teaching career, but I was ready to move on to a new adventure, so in 1962, I applied with the Department of Defense to teach in an Army school, specifying my preference for Germany or Japan.

"ARMY BRATS?"

Each major service: Army, Navy, and Air Force, recruited teachers separately during that time, though today, they all operate under the umbrella of the Armed Forces. I specified desirable locations. Besides Germany and Japan, I chose the Netherlands as a third possibility, but knew that there was only one base in that country.

After sending in my application, I was invited for an interview in a Seattle recruiting office. Since I had taught junior high my first three years, I asked for that level, and I knew I had a much greater chance of being placed where I wanted. So I was elated when I received an assignment in Germany.

My maternal grandparents lived in the Netherlands, and this would give me an opportunity to visit them often. Besides, the prospect of touring Europe from such a central location appealed to me. I was given a position in Hanau, a half-hour train ride from Frankfurt, a major hub.

My living quarters were in a Bachelor Officers Quarters, an apartment building that also housed lieutenants and other officers with similar ranks. Teachers were rated, and paid, as G-7s.

I shared a bathroom with another teacher, and we had a common hallway and front door. I had taken along all my belongings in my two trunks and a few suitcases, and I felt somewhat crowded in the small room.

I arrived a week before school was to begin, so I took my first train ride to see my grandparents, who had eagerly been awaiting my visit. I transferred in the huge Frankfurt station and caught a train to Amsterdam, a direct ride that stopped in Arnhem, my home town. I had not seen Oma and Opa for fourteen years, and we shed tears of joy.

I settled into my new teaching job. I liked the school: a one-story building with large windows, and my classroom was flooded with friendly light. From the first day, the children in my three seventh-grade classes were cooperative and pleasant, and we all had a smooth start.

However, I received an offer, as did another teacher, to transfer to Frankfurt Junior High. That school was short two teachers and were using substitutes. I thought about it. I would be even closer to my destination in the Netherlands, and the prospect of living in a large, exciting city appealed to me. Hanau was a lovely small community, but rather limited in interesting places to visit and good restaurants.

So three weeks after I had started at the Hanau school, the Army packed up my belongings again and moved me to a BOQ on one of several bases in Frankfurt. I was happy with my much larger room, and the view from the fourth floor afforded me a vista of German rooftops, a park, a lot of greenery, and a lot of sky.

My new roommate, Winnie, and I were both graduates from the University of Michigan, she a year ahead of me. Her best friend was Willa, and the three of us would spend a lot of time together, traveling and going out for dinners.

I arrived at my new school on Thursday, hitching a ride with another teacher who lived in the same building and taught in the same school. The school was housed in a former warehouse for German army tanks which used to be stored on the first floor, but now, the space had been partitioned into classrooms. In the middle of each classroom stood a reinforcement post, a column about eighteen inches square. The rooms were crowded with thirty to thirty-five desks, and some of these had to be behind the post and out of view of the teacher.

I was assigned a 7th grade class for the first two periods, a divided 8th grade before and after lunch, and another 8th the last two hours. Students arrived by bus from areas of Frankfurt, since American bases were scattered all over the city. This took a considerable amount of time out of children's days, particularly for those who lived far away.

My new students had had substitutes for the first three weeks of school, difficult for them, as well as for me. The first and last groups settled down right away and seemed relieved and glad when they learned that I would be their permanent English-Social Studies teacher for the year.

The group that met before and after lunch? Well, that was another matter. Other teachers had already warned me about this bunch; each of the classes stayed together throughout the day, with a math teacher, science, PE, and music. And they all had difficulty with this group, but nothing like what I endured the next few weeks.

When they arrived, they were shouting at each other, punching, laughing, running. I told them to pipe down, but I might as well have not been there at all. They paid not the slightest attention to me, except for the most irritating boy inn the class. He shouted at me, "Hey, Teach!," then stuck his forefingers in his mouth and pulled up the corners into a weird grin.

I wanted the first session to be about them, as I had in the other two classes, learning their names through playing a game and getting to know something about each student, but I soon saw that this would not happen with these kids.

I tried to not show my nervousness, but that is hard to hide from thirteen-year-olds, who love the idea of upsetting a teacher, if they can get away with it: at least, this was the group mentality of that class. They had received social studies books from one of the substitutes, so I wrote an assignment down on the board, indicating that they were to write out answers and hand those in the next day. Then, I walked around and talked to each of the students individually, asking their names.

Most were cooperative, but a half dozen or so, and it only takes that many, had great fun at my expense and said goofy names – literally, since one boy said he was "Goofy." I was too rattled to give that a snarky retort. Giving up finally, I sat down at my new desk and started looking over papers I had collected from my first class. I tried to ignore the kids as much as possible, praying that they would not kill each other, but I could only do that a few minutes, as I tried again to make my voice heard over the din.

During the lunch hour, I sought out the vice-principal, and found that he was well aware of the class. He had tried to intervene, he admitted, with several of the substitutes. He finally said, "Just ignore them. I'll pop in from time to time if I can."

I took him at his word. For that period after lunch, I did completely ignore them, though I was churning inside. Several students came up and asked if they could sit closer to the front so they could get some work done. I did that for them gladly, of course.

When I arrived the following day, I could see right away that nothing had changed. The handful of mostly boys were just as obnoxious and disruptive as the day before. I wrote an assignment down on the board and sat down to do paperwork. This time, I was a bit more relaxed, because I felt that the vice-principal had assumed some of the responsibility. More children asked if they could sit where there was less noise, and by the end of the two hours, the unruly kids pretty much occupied the back of the room, realizing that they were now being ignored by most of the class. They had lost at least part of their audience, but were having quite a lark among themselves.

The vice-principal walked by the room. I had purposely left the door open for all to hear the din. He came in and said, "How is everything going?"

I smiled broadly. "Oh, just fine, Mr. Moriarty." I really had relaxed more, and almost believed my own words, but it was a difficult two hours.

The next day was Saturday, and I welcomed the weekend break. I took a boat trip on the Main River, but could hardly enjoy it because of my worry about that class. If I could have gotten on a plane back to Seattle and forget that I had ever come, I would have been tempted to do so. I simply did not know the answer to my dilemma. I had heard the term, "Army Brats," referring to the children of the Military. Was this really true? Well, I could name several. The phrase that stood out in my memory was the one that had been shouted at me from a true "Army Brat" – *"Hey, Teach!"*

It occurred to me there were two ways to interpret that phrase. Was it a taunt, or a command? I decided to see it as the latter. I would teach!

Monday morning arrived. I stood by the door to greet the students of that class, but I noticed a change. Most sat down quietly and looked at me warily. I suspected a trick: something they had planned on a bus or in another class, but by now, they could hear every word I said. I wrote down a third assignment, then told the group, "If you are ready to learn, I am ready to teach." They stared at me, as if not knowing what to expect.

"I want all three assignments by tomorrow, or the first three marks in my record book will be *F*'s."

This spoke to most of them. They were, after all, Army children, and their parents were career officers of various ranks. A bad report on their children reflected on them, and the kids knew it. They grumbled, though, and said they had other homework, too, and how could they possibly get all of this done?

By this time, I had singled out three main perpetrators and sent them to the office one by one, to confront Mr. Moriarty. I had pre-arranged these meetings, and he knew enough about the kids from other teachers that he was glad to deal with them. All became cooperative, except for one boy. I took pains to ignore him and realized the other students were more than happy to do this, too. He gave every teacher grief and was given a warning, as were his parents. But he never did settle down, and a few weeks later, the whole family was sent back to the States. That was a threat that hung over every military family.

During the next days, I was stern and piled on a lot of work. It was not time to let up at all, and I knew it. Some students were furious with me and went to the counselor to complain, and to ask to be enrolled in another class. The counselor shared this with me. I told him he was welcome to come and talk to the class. He did arrive the next day, and I waited outside.

The class disrupted. The students were back to their yelling and running around, and I could also hear angry voices telling him what they thought of me, and how they wanted to be transferred. He came back outside, rattled, and said, "You've got to do something. Those kids hate you."

"Oh," I told him, "I'm *sooo* glad to hear that. And I don't want you to transfer anyone. They all have to stay."

He shook his head and walked away. I went back into the "lion's den," and they suddenly quieted down. "I'm staying, and so are all of you, so let's settle down and make this work," I told them. "And now, I have a story to read to you."

I don't remember the story, but it was something I had shared with my other classes, who had enjoyed it and it had engendered several good discussions.

It was a treat to them, after days of tension. In the weeks that followed, they mellowed, and so did I, and by the time half the year was over, they were my favorite class. Much of that cut-up behavior was eighth grade adolescent humor. Channeled, it was fun, and I encouraged it. They turned out to be some of the most creative kids I have ever taught, and several blossomed into good writers and conversationalists.

"Army brats?" Well, maybe a few, no more than anywhere else. One of the qualities I enjoyed about the children of Army personel was their flexibility. Their parents were often transferred to other parts of the world, and the children had to be enrolled during the school year. I was amazed at how well they adjusted and made new friends with ease. Some had lived in several countries, and their maturity reflected this.

During winter and spring breaks, I traveled or visited my grandparents. On weekends, I often went somewhere with various friends who lived in my BOQ. From Frankfurt, by train or car, we could reach Austria, Luxemburg, Belgium, France, the Netherlands, Switzerland, Lichtenstein, and Italy, as well as northern Germany, and we often left as soon as school was out on Friday, our bags already with us, to see as much as possible.

I took many pictures on my Canon. This was long before cell phone cameras, but slides greatly enhanced my teaching from then on, especially if I were teaching world geography. One Christmas vacation, I went on a Mediterranean cruise and visited eight countries and a Greek island. During the summers, I toured Scandanavia, the British Isles, and Italy with friends. One spring break, twenty of us went by tour bus and *Aeroflot* – the Soviet airline – and made stops in Prague, Warsaw, Minsk, Moscow, and Leningrad. On my own, I explored the land of my birth, The Netherlands.

I stayed in that school for two years. I was, by now, a "veteran" teacher, having established friendships with a number of my colleagues. We also had a new principal, and that second year needs a story of its own.

SECOND YEAR IN FRANKFURT

Although my classes that first year had settled down and become fun to teach, our school had a reputation of being the "roughest Army school in all of Europe," a dubious distinction that many on our staff seemed to be proud of. I must admit, I felt a sense of pride, too. After all, I had survived the year and decided to remain.

We had control of our students while they were in our classrooms, but the kids' behaviors on the buses was another matter. All children were bused in and the buses were driving by German Nationals, most of whom spoke little English. None took responsibility for what happened inside his bus, as long as their charges got to school on time. So when the kids arrived, they often reeked of cigarette smoke, and some were even under the influence of booze in smuggled flasks.

Since there were students from seventh through ninth grades on the buses, the discrepancy in size and maturity went from small prepubescent children to strapping youths in the prime hormonal stage in their lives. On several buses, the older boys would pick on a meek little child and "de-pants" him, to the delight of some of their friends, but to the horror of other children. The victim would not dare tell his parents and there seemed to be a code of secrecy among the other bus riders.

The principal and vice-principal, prodded by threats and anger from parents, would lecture a busload of kids occasionally, and ban someone from a bus from time to time, even expel the worst perpetrators, and the problems would stop for a while, only to show up a month or so later.

Enter Mr. Christiansen, the new principal the following year. He was a giant of a man, who could use his bulk to intimidate, or be protective and kind. At our first faculty meeting, he told us that he had stood in line at our PX check-out counter and had heard several teachers brag about our reputation. He told us emphatically that he never wanted to hear this again. We all cowered a little under his warning stance, but appreciated the perimeters he set on us, and on our students.

On the first day of school, the halls were a-buzz with talk about our new leader. Seems the Great Dane had boarded one of the buses and introduced himself to all the students. The next day, he showed up on another. In the weeks that followed, he picked each bus at random, often in the middle of the run, until he had ridden all of them. On each, he walked around and talked to the students, showing an interest in their lives. Needless to say, the problems on the buses were alleviated.

The physical make-up of the building also presented problems. The looming presence of the post in the middle of each room made it possible for kids to hide, and to write graffiti on the back of the beams. That activity was thwarted with buckets of soapy water and a forfeited lunch hour, imposed upon the perpetrators.

The burden for us, the faculty, had been that we had to spend the first part of the lunch hour with students eating in the classroom. There was no cafeteria. The the children had to bring their own lunches, and we had to make sure the room was clean again before the fifth period kids arrived.

The building had a huge attic, one half of which had been converted into a gymnasium, and we had suggested we use the other part as a lunchroom, but this was considered unsanitary. The ceiling loomed some thirty or forty feet above, and dust that lay in blobs on the rafters often dropped down and plopped on the floir and furniture, even on students.

Two faculty members came up with a brilliant solution. This was, after all, post-war Germany. World War II had ended less than twenty years ago, and many artifacts were in possession of German citizens. So the teachers put out a request for used parachutes. They knew there had to be thousands of them. They obtained about a dozen in various colors, and, putting up scaffolding, spanned the parachutes between posts and under the rafters. The result was quite dramatic and colorful. It solved the problem, and now, at least, the students could eat at long tables in the attic.

I had a ninth grade class that year that met the third hour and again the fifth, right after lunch. My curriculum included English and social studies, which meant world history at that level. I was teaching a unit about the Soviet Union at this time, with emphasis on the Cold War.

I found a fictitious story to read to my students, about a Soviet third grade class, who was asked by their teacher what they believed in. Most of them expressed a belief in God. So the teacher asked them to put their heads down on their desks and pray to God for candy. When told to look up, they found no candy on their desks. So this time, the teacher instructed them to pray to Khrushchev. She walked stealthily around the room and placed candy on each desk. Loyalties changed in an instant. Lesson learned.

My students were appalled. How could these kids be taken in so easily, just to get a reward? We had a lively discussion, and then I had a sudden flash of inspiration. I asked them to take out a piece of paper and number the lines from one to twelve. I told them to memorize the "facts" I was about the give them.

"Two plus two equals five," I told them. "Red and blue paint, mixed, produces the color, *orange*. Ancient people had three arms and three legs. Berlin is the capital of Denmark."

And so on. They became squirmy and some voiced their objections loudly. I ignored them, and then told them I was going to give them a quiz. They were to write down the answers as I had given them. I went over each of the "facts" again, as they quickly jotted down the answers – all except Rudy. He slouched in his chair and glared at me, tapping his pencil on the desk. When the rest of the class handed me their papers as they filed out for lunch, he slapped his blank sheet on my desk and stalked out of the room.

The students had a lunch hour to think about this, and must have told a number of their friends what had happened. Meanwhile, I stewed over my rash move to surprise them, and me, with what I had done. I was a bit nervous about it. All the students had answered all of the questions "correctly." Except for Rudy.

When they returned for the fifth period, someone else showed up, as well: Mr. Christianson. Ooops! Word had gotten to him, apparently. They sat down, many with belligerent expressions on their faces. I told them to relax – they had all done perfect papers, and all earned A's, except for Rudy. He had received an F, because he had turned in a blank paper.

My students were outraged. They said it was not fair at all to Rudy.

I reassured them. I had not recorded any grades in my grade book, because I wanted to discuss this with them. Should I write them in, or not? Most decided that they wanted the A's. but that Rudy should receive one, too, because he had been the only person with enough integrity to forfeit a grade. I told them that it didn't work that way. All the grades would be listed as marked, or we would toss out all the papers.

One girl spoke. "This is like those kids with the candy, isn't it? We were just as willing to go against what we believed in order to get a perfect grade."

Light dawned on more of the students, as they realized what they had done. Someone suggested that Rudy should receive an A, and the rest, take the consequences of getting an F.

We finally decided, as did Rudy, to throw out the papers. Lesson learned.

Christiansen congratulated me. "I honestly had no idea how you were going to get out of that one."

"Neither did I," I confessed. "But I think they got the point."

TEACHING IN MY OLD HIGH SCHOOL

At the end of my second year of teaching for the Army in Germany, I had to make a decision. Was I to remain at Frankfurt Junior High, where I had become comfortable and satisfied? Should I stay in Frankfurt, an exciting city which I had learned to master somewhat, and also remain near my grandparents in the Netherlands? Should I apply for an assignment in another country? Some of my friends wanted to spend a couple of years at US bases in Japan, and that seemed exciting.

I felt that if I stayed with the DOD (Department of Defense) system one more year, I would be hooked forever, and become an expat. Besides, I wanted to get re-acquainted with my parents. I had lived far away from them for five years, so I decided to go back to Grand Rapids and trust that I could find a job. After all, I was still interested in junior high, and that was an age that most did not want to teach.

My first action, once I was in the town of my growing-up years, was to go to the Education Administration building and apply. To my surprise, I was interviewed by Mr. Sherman, former football coach at my high school, now on the District's staff.

I felt he fitted this role much better than that of a tenth grade world history teacher. I remember being bored in his classroom, while most of the girls sat and stared at him, enraptured. He was, after all, a hunk, according to them. He spent many a session leaning back in his chair, feet on the desk, arms behind his head, telling one of two stories: a memorable football game in his coaching career, or the time he spent summer vacations driving an eccentric old man around the United States.

The boys enjoyed the football stories, but I tried to extrapolate some meaning out of the chauffeuring trips he took. Rather than talking about the Grand Canyon or Mount Rushmore, which might at least have been interesting, he told of the difficulties he had with his employer. For instance, the guy loved the Walt Disney movie, *Fantasia*, and he, Mr. Sherman, had to sit through the movie in every theater where it played. Such suffering!

As a tenth grade student, I had felt disdain for the handsome bore, and I often brought my knitting to class, clicking away rudely. When he reprimanded me once, I told him I would put away the knitting as soon as he had something worthwhile to say. He never challenged me again.

Therefore, I was somewhat apprehensive when I saw him sitting there, in the Administration Building, ten years older, while my future was in his hands. However, he was most pleasant, remembered me as one of his favorite (the liar!) students, and asked if I would like to teach at South High.

So that's how I, with mixed emotions, ended back in my old high school, but I did enjoy that year. Many of the staff were still there. Miss Shepard, the stunning middle-aged counselor of my student years, was now the principal, with beautifully coiffured white hair. I was supposed to call her Marjorie, but I'm not sure I ever did. Mike Murphy, the basketball coach, had been my seventh-grade geography teacher, and I had loved that class. It seemed strange to call Mr. Murphy by his first name now. He was glad to see me as a colleague, and he and his wife invited me over for dinner several times.

South was both junior and senior high, and I had three seventh-grade classes and two tenth grade. During the time that I was a student, the population had been 75% Caucasian and 25% black. Now, it was 55% black.

I soon learned not to enter the staff lunchroom, because a number of teachers talked loudly with racial slurs about the students they were teaching. I noticed, also, that Mike Murphy never spent time there. I ate either in my classroom, or, on nice days, drove to a nearby park, opened the sun roof of my VW, and read a book.

One of the tenth grade classes, which met right after lunch, was all black. Several of the students were veterans from the Vietnam War, which was still raging at the time. They had done their two years of service, then returned to school to earn their high school degree.heading One of the vets, Eddie, called me "Teach," and was only few years younger than I, would smile and wink at me, but I saw it as good-natured. I'm not sure if he ever took me seriously. And why should he? I was too naïve to fully understand what he might have experienced during his service time.

My mind went back to the class in Germany, and that truly malicious child that blurted out: "Hey, Teach." Now, hearing it from Eddie, I smiled and thought, *You bet. I teach.*

I don't know how much that class learned from me about grammar, literature, and writing, but I learned a lot from them. The first few days, they came in orderly and sat down to listen, but then, when they became more familiar with each other, several would enter and say, "Hi," then use the N word to friends across the room. I put up with it for a day or so, but then asked them to stop using it.

"Aw, we don't mean anything by it. Nobody gets insulted."

"But I feel insulted for you," I told them. "It makes me uncomfortable to hear you say that word. Am I at liberty to call you that?"

Well, certainly not, they told me.

"Then, what you call each other outside of this classroom is none of my business, but in here, I do not want to hear word again."

My students got the message and respected my demand. I silently breathed a sigh of relief, and my respect for them shot way up. One day, Eddie, who had never participated in this name calling, came in, singing, "Trailers for sale or rent, rooms to let fifty cents." The song had just been released and was a national hit.

I chuckled as he continued to saunter toward his place: "I'm a man of means by no means," plopping into his seat, "King of the road!" By the next day, it had become the entry march of the class.

These students taught me a lot about the black culture in Grand Rapids. The school year, 1964-1965, was just before the Watts upheaval, so blacks were still referred to as Negroes. The Grand Rapids Negroes, my students told me, were divided between the Ottawa High Negroes and the South High. The Ottawa students were children of professionals: doctors, lawyers, teachers, while the parents of the South kids worked in factories and restaurants, but certainly employed. The South Negroes lived either east of Division Avenue or west. Those west were much poorer: broken families, parents often unemployed. I knew that was true, also, of the white people who lived in this west side. They went on to tell me that the West side was again a division between the Hill Toppers and the Black Bottoms, and they advised me never to drive through the Black Bottom area by myself. But, they also said, that when there was a party in the Black Bottom region, Negro kids from everywhere would come, because that is where the booze was, and the women, and the police were not likely to show up.

Toward the end of the year, several students invited me to be a chaperone at the Sophomore Prom. When I arrived, I found that I was the only white person in the room. I did not realize that white kids did not attend the proms anymore, as we had in my high school days. The other chaperones were parents of the children. They all greeted me warmly, and I felt honored to have been invited.

My other 10th grade English class was much different from the first. Labeled an "Honors Class," many of the students had graduated from Burton Junior High, a school in an affluent suburb of Grand Rapids.

I remembered this influx from my own experience as a student. I was comfortable with my junior high years at South, with a mixed racial and economic population. The sudden invasion of girls in cashmere sweater sets, new saddle shoes, and confident socialite behaviors, left me reeling and uncertain. I watched them try out and get accepted into the cheerleading squad. However, I was able to hold my own academically, so I soon got used to the changes.

And here they were again, the Burton kids, this time dominating my Honors Class. After all, they had had more opportunity to excel in school work than the six-year South students.

We had academic traditions in the English department that had gone through little change since I had attended. All students were given a *Memory Selections* book at the beginning of their career at South. The book contained about a half dozen poems or prose for each grade level, that were to be committed to memory. These included: "The Gettysburg Address," "To a Daffodil," "Ozymandias." As a student, I loved learning them.

We were each required to stand in front of the class and recite the assigned poems throughout the year. I remembered being afraid, and yet loving to master and perform each selection.

I've been grateful, all my life, for this discipline that was forced upon me by my various English teachers, and I wanted to instill this into these classes. The Honors Class enjoyed the challenge. The 5th period group was less than enthusiastic, and I encouraged them to find selections in black literature that they could share with ther class. One girl pursued this enthusiastically, finding quotes from Langston Hughes and Maya Angelou.

Something else that had not changed was the required teaching of at least two prescribed pieces of literature: *Macbeth* and *Silas Marner*.

I remembered reading *Silas Marner* in my own 10th grade class, and I had not liked it. How would these students, in many ways more modern and sophisticated than I was at their age, take to this?

So I told them the truth: "I did not enjoy *Silas Marner* when I had to read it, but I am required to teach it to you." I did explain that the author had used a pseudonym, because, during the era that she wrote her novels, women authors were not taken seriously.

To my surprise, a number of people in the class took this as a challenge and checked out the books way before they needed to. After a few days, several came back to tell me how much they liked the story.

I was amazed and decided to run with it. I tossed my arms outward in a show of incredulity. "How can you possibly enjoy it? It's so stilted."

More students took copies home. They were going to prove me wrong, and in a sense, ganged up on me with their arguments. I started to "come round" more and more as one girl told me how much she empathized with the old man, and how shocked and sad she was when his gold was stolen. Some even went to the library to learn more about weaving and daily life during that time in the 18ᵗʰ Century.

What happened next was one of my most satisfying moments in my teaching: The students, not I, decided to put a magazine together, and name it *The Raveloe Review*, after the name of Silas Marner's town in England. They elected an editor and included stories of people in the town and the tragedy of Silas' loss. They explained the miraculous appearance at his doorstep of a small child with golden hair. Some drew advertisements of clothing items, weaving looms, farm implements, and homes for sale.

As in all schools at the time, we had a mimeograph machine, so I made a few purple and white copies of the magazine, but not all students were able to have one. For a while, I kept the original with its colored pencil illustrations, but sadly, I have lost that.

I have a special affinity for that classic novel now, and I hope it was the beginning for a number of those creative students into learning to appreciate English authors, particularly, George Eliot.

Reflecting back on this teaching experience at my old high school, I feel a certain sadness, even though at the time, I coped reasonably well. I noticed the changes between my student days at South and my teaching experience there. During the time I attended, I don't remember much animosity between Caucasian and black students. True, the children of color tended to associate with whom they felt most familiar, but we had blacks on the Student Council and on the football team. Our class homecoming king was black. I was relatively unaware of problems that brewed, partly because of my naïvetee and partly because I chose not to see them. During those years in the fifties, people of the two ethnic groups were aware of their "place" in society and did not question those positions nearly as much as we all did in later years. Under the surface of relative politeness, a tempest was probably brewing, and by the time I taught at South ten years later, it was about to explode. Perhaps the animosity had been there, but as a teenager, I remember those six student years with great fondness, and though most of my friends were white, I got along fine with black classmates.

I arrived at South as a teacher, after having been away for ten years. I recognized many on the staff who had been there when I had been a student, including the counselor, who was now an aging principal, close to retirement. They were not nearly as aware that the student population had changed. With rare exceptions, like my friend Mr. Murphy, most were stuck in their comfortable niches, teaching their subject material in much the same way as they always had. They might have grown bitter and bored. Most were looking forward to retirement, and there were rumors, which later proved to be true, that South High would no longer exist in five years.

Was I racially biased while I was a teacher at South? If so, I was not aware of it then. In fact, it took another ten years or so to fully grasp hold of the extent of my tolerance and lack thereof. A Seattle workshop in race relations finally convinced me, and everyone else in the group, that we were prejudiced. Never mind the good friendships I had with a number of people of color, or that African American parents seemed to trust me. Whenever I hear someone say that he or she is not prejudiced, I realize that person has not reached that level of awareness to realize they can feel safe in ordinary situations that black people need to fear.

Even now, I am becoming more aware of how I take "white privilege" for granted.

I yearned to go back to the Northwest. I had reacquainted myself with the daily life of my parents and I lived in an apartment nearby, but had not made many friends on the faculty. I did not feel at home with my old high school friends anymore. Our lives had become so different. So I packed up my belongings and told my parents I was going back to my favorite area of the world.

RAINIER BEACH JUNIOR-SENIOR HIGH

My father suggested that he accompany me on the Trans-Canadian Highway, my chosen route, to help drive my red Volkswagen. I eagerly accepted. This would be a chance for him and me to become acquainted with each other as friends. Mother usually dominated conversations between the three of us, but this way, Dad and I could develop our own relationship.

Everything turned out as I had planned: Dad and I had a great journey, with sight-seeing side trips. We stayed with friends in Edmonds. I drove Dad to the airport, where he took his first flight in a plane larger than a pre-World War II four-seater. I found an apartment with Lake Union as my front yard, and I was offered a job at a nearly-new school: Rainier Beach Junior-Senior High.

As before, my teaching assignment would be seventh grade English and social studies. By this time, I was a veteran with that age and those familiar subjects. But as always, I prepared new material, and once I got to know my classes, I adjusted my lesson plans to fit individual groups.

Rainier Beach was experiencing rapid student population growth. The modern one-level brick building was no longer adequate to house all the students, so I was assigned to one of the half dozen portables behind the building

The faculty, younger and much more innovative than the teachers at South, reminded me more of my colleagues at Frankfurt Junior High. An active *Visual Aids* department, run by juniors and seniors, was experimenting with closed-circuit television, and I wondered how I, a mere seventh-grade teacher, could make use of this technology. Each classroom had a television fastened high on the wall, and various programs were regularly shown, as well as ads for up-coming school events, both sports and academic.

Besides the usual grammar, history and literature requirements, I would be teaching a unit on Greek mythology. I mulled over how to make this as interesting as possible, and came up with an idea – not after weeks of planning, but quite on the spur of the moment.

While giving a test on adverbs one day, I felt driven to go to the blackboard and write down the names of each of my students. Next to each, I wrote the name of a Greek god or goddess. Curious, someone asked what this was for. I ignored the question. I had left space next to each Greek to add a name of people in my second class, so when they came in, they were met with the same mystery.

The next day, when my first class walked in, one boy said, "I'm Narcissus, and I'm very, very handsome!"

The rest of the class groaned, and a girl grumbled, "Yeah, I'm Echo, and you dumped me, you stuck-up brat!"

Patrick said, "Don't worry, Echo. I'm Zeus, and I like all women, even you."

"That's for sure," complained 'Hera.' "You're the worst cheating husband anyone ever had."

I had a hard time containing my excitement. I realized my students had gone to the library on their own to find the information.

I asked them to open their grammar books, but looked forward to the following week, when we would plunge into this romp with the Greeks. By the time Monday arrived, every student not only knew his or her own identity, but that of most of the classmates.

The student texts for this unit were lively and engaging, but even more interesting now because of the personal connections. I felt dialog could add more humor, so I wrote a play and included parts for all the students. I wrote choruses to be performed by a speaking choir, as well. At first, I had just planned for them to read the parts, but they wanted to memorize their lines. I showed the play to the Visual Aids faculty member, and she wanted me to work this into a half hour performance, to be televised to the student body.

Two of my classes wanted to perform, so I adjusted parts and made sure that anyone who wished, could be in the play. Parents became involved, making costumes.

We fashioned and painted props, including a cardboard expanse of waves that could be moved up and down and sideways. We practiced every day, first in the classroom, and toward the imminent day of the performance, the Visual Aids staff member and students practiced filming us. On the Saturday before the play was to be aired, we all came in and put it together.

The following week, on a designated day, the thirty-minute skit, *Pardon Me, Your Mortality is Showing*, was featured in every English class, from the seventh-graders to Seniors. Some, I understand, laughed *at* my kids, and some, *with* them. For a few weeks, my adolescents were stars, often recognized and praised in the halls by older students. And I admit, I enjoyed my "stardom," too. After all, I had given each English teacher a day off from having to make lesson plans. And it was actually a very funny play, with references to music and current TV shows, like *Laugh-In*.

I spent three years at "the Beach," ending, finally, with several 11th grade English classes. By now, in my career, I had taught every junior and senior high level, except for seniors, though I was in charge of a senior home room that third year.

When anyone asks me what level I enjoyed the most, I could honestly say I liked seventh graders the best, but also tenth graders. Seventh graders were still young adolescents who needed to feel cared about and safe, and tenth graders were coming to the realization that they were becoming adults. My challenge was to encourage those 16-year-old young people to stay in school and help them to see that having a high school degree was important. I was sad each time someone dropped out of school when he or she turned sixteen.

By the time students reached eleventh grade, they were there to get decent grades that would help them to graduate and/or go to college. I was amazed at first that when I asked them to open their books, they did so without squirming or dawdling, or telling me they had forgotten their materials. They turned in papers on time, studied for tests, and were courteous and pleasant. They were easier to teach, but I felt they were not as attached to me personally. They would have done this for any teacher. So my challenge was to set up interesting discussions around the subject material, which, if I remember from that time, was the study of American literature.

What I think back on most from those three years were the seventh graders that first year, and the play we put together. I wanted to imagine that they would remember Greek mythology for much of their lives.

AN ALL-BOYS CLASS

At the end of the third year at Rainier Beach, I was offered the position as Head of the English Department in Wilson Junior High School. This would mean an extra stipend in my salary, and a new experience.

I had become comfortable at "The Beach," and I felt like an established teacher. This might have been enough to keep me settled in, but opportunity for higher salary and a more prestigious position as department head was enough incentive to move me on to my next teaching venture.

Wilson Junior High had a stern and autocratic principal, but I soon found out that the teaching staff had ways of working around him. The vice principal and counselor were more approachable.

I was assigned two eighth-grade English-social studies combinations, and my 3rd period was a seventh-grade English class.

I settled into my new position without much difficulty, but did find the 7th graders challenging, because of three or four students that were willful and disruptive. This kind of behavior was not new to me, but the rest of the class was pleasant, so I worked around the problems as best I could.

I soon learned that all second periods were 7th grade English classes. I started to hear complaints from other teachers, that those particular groups were suffering because of several students in each class that they found impossible to work with. It was ruining their ability to reach the rest of the kids.

Most of these youngsters, mainly boys, had come from the same school, where they had run rough-shod over their teachers: in fact, each grade level that these children passed through, had been difficult.

I listened to the complaints and offered a solution. Each of our five classes consisted of twenty-six or twenty-seven students. I asked each teacher to pick out the three most annoying troublemakers, and I would take them the second semester. These I would exchange for five of my students, but keep three of my own. This meant that I would have a classroom of fifteen students, and theirs would be in the high twenties. I said that I wanted only boys, thus breaking one of my own teaching rules: Treat boys and girls equally.

By this time, I had taught this grade level long enough to know that the boys were often still children with voices that would slip between high and low notes, embarrassing to them. Their faces, still smooth, had to look up to their girl classmates, since that spurt of growth that they would develop two years later, had not yet happened.

Most of the girls had reached puberty, with body changes that were driving the smaller boys a bit crazy. They could not attract the females with their virility, so they often tried to make up for it with strange antics.

The age range from twelve to fourteen is difficult for all new teens, but it is particularly tough for boys. I figured that without the distraction of female hormones, the boys might be more focused on being students.

When my small class showed up in late January, they looked around and discovered that all their best buddies were in the same class. What fun! They shouted at each other, threw wads of paper, made weird faces at me, and giggled, turning around in their seats to make clever and lewd comments.

I asked each for his name. The first offers were real. Then someone said, "Elvis Presley," while brushing back his hair, getting up and gyrating for the benefit of the others. I could not allow him to take control. I knew I had to do something drastic immediately.

I had worked out a plan with the vice principal, so I knew I had a back-up. I wrote out a hall pass and sent the young buck to the office. I realized I was about to break a second rule in working with kids: I did not believe in corporal punishment. At the time, this was still allowed in the schools, and I knew that Mr. Olson used it sparingly.

Another boy turned out to be Donald Duck and quacked loudly, to the great glee of the class. I sent him out, too, just as Glen, aka Elvis, was returning and with a painful grimace, eased himself into his seat. Soon, "Donald" waddled in and sat down carefully.

A sullen silence descended upon the group. I handed out books, sheets of lined paper, and pencils, and told them to copy spelling words I had written on the blackboard. Most obeyed, though some slouched in their chairs, arms folded and glared at me. I would give them a test on Friday. I had purposely made the words very easy, and told them that anyone who got half of them correct, would get a C, thirteen right would be a B, and sixteen, an A. It was generous, and they knew it. What kind of a fool was this teacher, anyway?

I explained that I would give a weekly grade for everything else. Turn in four other assignments each week, and this would be an *A*. Three, a *B*, Two a *C*, and anything less, unacceptable. They did not have to take the work home. There would be plenty of time to finish it in class. It would consist of writing answers to questions they could look up in their reading books, a short grammar assignment, a couple of sentences that they would write about a topic, and a joke or a poem or a magazine ad that they would share with the class. Quality would not be graded. All that mattered was that they hand in the papers.

I was about to break a third principle: Grade on quality. Make students strive for it. Yet here I was, practically encouraging sloppy work.

Each day that week, I handed out paper and pencils, since the boys did not bring these items themselves. I assigned one of the easy lessons, and when they were finished, they could choose a book or a game to stay busy. Some got right to it, others sat and looked out the window or tried to get the attention of a friend across the room. The classroom atmosphere was orderly but just barely.

On Friday, I gave the spelling test. I corrected them quickly and handed them back with a grade. I counted up the other papers each had handed in, and found that four of the students had earned an A for the week. They were astounded at how easy this was. For some, it had been the first "A" they had ever received in all their schooling. This teacher was, indeed, a bit crazy. Most knew they had not done "A" work.

The following week, the assignments were similar, but I made each a bit more demanding. More kids cooperated. The room was relatively quiet with their activity, which gave me a chance to sit down with each individual some time during the week, and get to know him better: Who were his friends? Brothers and sisters? What food did he like best? What was his favorite sport? Favorite team? What did he like to do at home when he had some free time? Could he write a few sentences about something? If a student did not know how to spell a certain word, he was free to ask me.

After three weeks, papers were coming in with more sentences, less mistakes. By now, most were turning in all their assignments. It was time to up the ante some more. But there were still boys who just couldn't care less.

While teaching in Germany, I had collected a number of posters of places I had been. I brought them to class. I told the students that anyone who could get three A's in three weeks, which would mean turning in all their assignments, could choose one. This went over beyond my expectation. They wanted posters!

Almost all were aboard now, except for Stan, who spent the class hours in sullen silence, staring out the window. Any attempt of mine to engage him in conversation, failed, and I chose to accept this behavior.

I was running out of posters and asked friends and colleagues for more. One day, I found a geophysical map of an area near Mount Rainier, and I displayed it. Stan's eyes lit up. "What is that?" he asked.

I explained to him about the contour lines and how he could figure out elevations and depressions by studying this map.

"Can I have it?" he asked.

"Sure. You know what you have to do to earn it."

For the next three weeks, Stan turned in all of his work, and his essay, one of the longest of that week, was about the map. The spelling was mostly correct, as well. I found another map of an area in the Olympics, and he earned that, too. We talked about the elevation in the two areas: the Olympics were closer to sea level, and the rock formations were entirely different. He never needed another poster, but he did his work from then on, and now, we had a lot to talk about. I had done some climbing a few years earlier, and we discussed camping and climbing gear. I don't know what his future turned out to be, but I'd like to think that it became brighter for him that semester.

The class was becoming more relaxed and trusting. I found a set of books with short skits. They enjoyed this, and often hammed up their parts. For some, reading was still difficult, but they were patient with each other.

We found a play we all liked, and they agreed to perform this for the other 7th grade English classes. I knew I was taking a chance: I wanted to enhance their self-esteem, not jeopardize it, so I sought the cooperation from the other teachers, who talked this up with their students. It turned out to be a fine success.

Meanwhile, something else was happening. The math, science, and art teachers were telling me that the boys were behaving well in their classes, doing their work, and getting decent grades.

I only spent that one year at Wilson, because I was awarded a grant to Arizona State for a Master's Degree in elementary counseling, so I was about to go through a career change.

I did keep in touch with Wilson's counselor, who told me that the boys continued to do average to good work during the rest of their stay at Wilson, and they were much pleasanter and happier people.

And, I figured, growing taller and being noticed and admired by girls would make a big difference!

MASTER'S DEGREE AT ASU

In April of 1969, the year I taught at Wilson, I applied for a US government grant to attend Arizona State University in their elementary counseling program. Though high school counselors had been employed for a long time, professional counseling for the lower grades was a relatively new idea, and its use was still being defined. The program seemed intriguing to me, and I wanted to be part of something that was still in the experimental stage.

The main function for high school counselors was to help students decide what to do with their lives, which often meant choosing a college or university that would meet their needs. This could also include talking to students about subjects they should be taking in their high school to prepare them for a specialized field, or to expedite scholarships and get them into college.

If you asked most high school counselors what they liked best about their jobs, they would likely tell you that this was talking to students and parents about personal and relationship problems. That's why they had majored in psychology in the first place. But so often, this kind of counseling was put on the back burner while the adjusting of class sizes, finding scholarships, helping students find appropriate higher education opportunities, and dealing with statistics of their schools, became as much as ninety percent of their jobs.

How should a counseling program for younger students be defined? This specialist could help facilitate relationships between students and teachers, students and other students, students and parents, and even principals and others in the school. This is what attracted me to this special government grant program. The program staff was looking to fill thirty positions. The year before, there had been two thousand applicants. My chances of getting in were slim, at best, but I decided to give it a try.

On the appointed day and time, I met with the director of the program. He seemed fleetingly interested in my resumé; after all, it had been the first stage of selecting applicants. His questions had to do with how I would handle certain situations as a teacher, what my basic teaching philosophy was in dealing with students, and why I thought I would qualify working with elementary-age children. After all, my teaching experience had only been with junior and senior high students.

Then, he launched into more personal questions. How would I feel about becoming like family with a group of thirty people? Would I participate a lot in social events?

I liked how this conversation was going, and I relaxed. I felt comfortable asking questions about his life, as well. We became more and more informal, as we "shot the breeze."

Toward the end of the interview, he asked "Do you think you are going to get in?"

The question caught me off guard, but only for a moment. I gave him a one-word answer: "Yes!"

I felt him studying me. "Why do you think so?"

"Because I want to," I told him.

A few weeks later, I received my acceptance into the program. When I met him again later that summer when classes began, he told me that this answer, "because I want to," was a deciding factor, for him.

I spent an extraordinary year at Arizona State. The emphasis of the Master's program was to become change agents in our schools, by systemically helping a school population, from principal, to parents, to teachers, to custodians, from youngest to oldest child – become focused on learning respect and trust – and feeling, which we now see as a hackneyed cliché, "good about themselves." Much as we might roll our eyes about that expression now, it is still a relevant ingredient for success at any level of education.

First of all, we had to expand ourselves to internalize that idea. So we were each assigned to a therapy group that we met with once a week. We had an extensive book list that we were encouraged to read, and much of our discussions took place after our morning classes, often over slices of pizza and pitcher of beer at one of the local pubs.

Spouses and children of our group members were invited to participate, and some of the wives formed discussion groups on their own. I'd like to say that none of these marriages were ever challenged that year, but that's not true. Since we were all encouraged to "change," this often happened to the wives more than to their husbands. Not all the marriages survived in the next few years.

Suffice it to say that we had a lot of parties, swam in a lot of pools, and shared the music of the 60'S decade – Leonard Cohen, Judy Collins, Cat Stevens, the Moody Blues, Joan Baez, Neil Diamond, Simon and Garfunkle, to name a few. And the staff participated in our social events.

I read a lot of philosophy and psychology, and I practiced my new counseling skills on undergraduate university students, who signed up for free services from us. We received our first clients six weeks after we were in their program, and I remember feeling terrified with the thought of that responsibility, but it turned out to be one of the most valuable things I did that year for my own learning, and I know it helped my clients, as well. We held these sessions in small booths with one-way glass, and we never knew when we might be observed by a staff member.

In the spring, as the program was winding down, we were assigned to elementary schools as student counselors. I worked mainly with a teacher and her second-grade class, and she was delighted by how the children enjoyed what we all did together. I met with individual students who were having their own problems, with small groups to give each child a chance to talk in a more intimate setting, and finally, the entire class with interesting exercises to help them know each other in a more personal way.

At the end of the year – one of the most pivotal of my life – I was ready to take on this new venture. Elementary Counseling was still an experimental program in Seattle Schools, and I had no trouble securing an assignment at Cooper, a Kindergarten through sixth grade school located in West Seattle.

COUNSELING AT COOPER

Armed with my year of counseling experiences at Arizona State University, I walked into my new job at Cooper Elementary School. Housed in a brick building from the 20's, this solid, no-nonsense structure teemed with 500 elementary students from Kindergarten through 6th grade. I was given a room half the size of a regular classroom, which pleased me, because it was not the stereotypical office with a desk chair and a large desk between my clients and me, but a space large enough for groups and activities. I brought in whatever pillows I could find and piled them in a corner, added a few stuffed animals, and hung up colorful posters.

The staff was eager to meet me. They had never worked with a counselor before, and were pleased that theirs was one of the schools that was selected for this still-experimental endeavor. The principal, Mr. Cranston, had committed his school to this new venture in Seattle Schools.

I explained that I was there in the traditional role of liaison between student and teacher, student and parent, student and principal, but also to aid teachers in learning counseling skills that they could use in the classroom and in conferences with parents.

They told me that the school population included key-latch children and many from broken homes. They were often difficult children to work with, because many were malnourished and not disciplined at home. They received school lunches, but often would arrive in the morning hungry.

This was a few years before mandatory busing, so most of the students walked to school. Classes were large, and teachers often felt that they could not reach some of their students as much as they wanted to. They looked forward to sending the really troubled kids to me.

This was their concept of a school counselor who did not have to spend time scheduling or working with colleges, but who was there merely to "fix" the difficult children and send them back to the classroom as more cooperative people.

Several teachers had no idea why I was necessary at all. They could take care of their own students just fine, thank you. If someone acted up, that child was sent to the principal, who would administer appropriate punishment when necessary. That's what kids needed – lots of discipline.

Mr. Cranston, with whom I became good friends, was stern, but would talk to students rather than use the paddle. He did not own a "board of education" that some principals still displayed prominently, as a joke: "Ha ha, but watch out."

When the students arrived a few days later, I helped the staff direct them to the right classrooms. The children, often timid on this first day, were orderly and reasonably quiet. The "new" kids were easy to spot and needed help in this formidable, no-nonsense building. Old friends greeted each other, and I wondered who was glad to be back, and who would have liked the summer to last a whole lot longer.

I figured that my first week was best used by roaming the hallways and talking to students on the playground during recess and lunch time. I also made an appointment with each teacher to visit his or her classroom. I wanted the students to call me "Mieke." This had been recommended to us in our ASU training. Some of the teachers were not happy with this, but it went over well with the girls and boys that I met that week.

After they learned who I was, I would often be approached by a child who broke out of line to give me a hug, yelling "Mieke!" Hugging, something most seemed to understand, was welcomed by me. Many teachers hugged their students, too. It was that time before hugging was suspected of being questionable behavior. I'm sorry that has become such an exaggerated issue now. Children need affection, which they often do not get it at home.

Some students asked to see me, and when parents found out about me, they made appointments, as well. But the majority of one-on-one sessions I had at first were initiated by teachers. "I'm having trouble with Marlene. Talk to her and send her back, so that she will fit into the class more easily." "Please talk to Larry and tell him that his weird behavior is not acceptable."

I soon heard about Ronald, the "most disturbed boy in the school," and the one who seemed to be responsible for more trouble than any one kid could possibly cause. If something was stolen or broken, it became a cliché that this fourth grader, Ronald, had done it. He was the most likely culprit, and in my mind, the scapegoat of the school, and the trouble had started the year before, when he had moved to the neighborhood.

I knew of Ronald, but had not met him personally until one day, as I was walking down the 2nd floor hall, I spied him sitting on the floor outside his classroom, slamming a softball from one hand to the other. Making children sit outside the classroom was apparently accepted as discipline in this school. I figured that his teacher had sent him there to get some relief from his behavior. I knew that Sandy had a difficult combination of students that year.

"Kind of lonesome out here, isn't it, Ronald?" I asked him.

Without looking up, he grunted something unintelligible.

"I'm having a bad day," I said. "Mind if I join you?"

Ronald shrugged.

I sat down next to him. "Want to talk about it?"

"Nah."

"OK," I said, and we sat quietly for a few minutes. I broke the silence. "You like to play softball?"

"I like baseball better."

"You play on a team?"

"I wish."

That seemed to be the end of the conversation, so we sat some more.

After a while, Ronald mumbled, "She hates me."

"Your teacher?"

"Yeah. I'm pretty bad in there."

"What happens?"

"Oh, I mouth off. That's what I did this time."

"Well, I imagine that would make her mad at you, all right."

"I don't mean to do it. It just comes out."

"I know you don't. I think you are really strong and can resist saying something when you get that urge."

Ronald pressed the softball between his hands. "Think so?"

"Would you like it if I went in with you and asked if you could be back in class?"

"I guess so."

I promised Sandy that Ronald wanted to give this another try. She grumbled her consent, then told me later I had had no right to interfere in this way. But could she send Ronald to me several times a week, so I could talk to him and get him to be better behaved?

I suggested an alternative. I wanted to meet with Ronald, but as part of a group of his classmates. I asked her to pick another child who was difficult, and also two good students that were well-liked by the others, as well as several who were quiet and hard to reach in a large classroom. As a teacher, I had often been most worried about the shy children who caused no trouble, but who were nearly invisible in a large group.

Sandy sent four boys and three girls, and I was thankful for the size of my room. We sat on a circle of pillows on the floor, which was a novelty to them. By this time, I had some rapport with Ronald. After all, we had already shared floor space the week before. I asked them general questions: what did they like to eat, what did they do after school, what was their favorite toy, did they have a pet, or would they like one? Each child had a chance to say as much as he or she wanted. In the weeks that followed, they learned to trust each other with much more personal stories: what scared them, what made them happy. I encouraged them to ask questions of each other, and I was amazed at how insightful some of these questions were. Ronald became good at it.

I suggested that we focus on each person for a few minutes and tell that boy or girl something we particularly liked about her or him. They were eager to give that a try, and it was gratifying to see their smiles, even some close to tears, when they absorbed the good things their friends were telling them.

Sandy told me that the atmosphere was improving in her classroom, and it was clear that the rest of the class looked up to the members of this special group. The shy children spoke up more in class, and the "popular" ones modeled behaviors that were catching on by others, such as asking them questions about themselves and showing empathy.

One day, when I was walking them back to their classroom, Ronald and another boy were tossing his ever-present softball back and forth between them. They often did this, and I thought nothing of it. But this particular day, we were going up the stairs when Ronald threw the ball too high, and it crashed through the window at the top of the stairwell between the first and second floors.

Ronald looked at me and gulped. We both said, "Oh, no!" at the same time.

"I'm so sorry, Ronald," I told him. "I should not have allowed you boys to play catch like that in the halls."

"But I threw the ball," he said. "It was my fault."

"What do you think we should do?" I asked him.

Ronald slumped his shoulders. "I have to tell Mr. Cranston."

"I want to go along," I told him. "It's my fault, too."

We went to see the Principal. Ronald told him, nervously, what he had done, and I added my role in this.

Frank Cranston, bless him, was equally stern with both of us, telling us that it was going to cost a lot of money to fix.

Ronald reached in his pocket and pulled out some change. "I've got fifty cents."

I reached in my purse. "And I've got five dollars."

Frank took my bill and then fished a quarter out of Ronald's palm. "You may need that other quarter, Ronald," he said. "This is plenty generous, and I thank you."

He made us promise to never do this again, and we solemnly gave him our word. I winked at Ronald, and he grinned back.

I had contact with Ronald's mother, and I knew she tried as best she could, but her family of five kids was an overwhelming responsibility for her. Theirs was a tough environment for a vulnerable ten-year-old child. I wish I had kept track of Ronald, but his family moved that summer, and we never saw him again.

There are many stories to tell about that school and the children. A few more stand out in my mind.

The sixth grade teacher hauled in two girls, practically by the scruff of their necks. They had been fighting, and she just didn't know what to do with them. Would I calm them down, please, and send them back? She left, without waiting for my answer.

The two girls resumed yelling at each other, and I could see they were close to blows again.

I picked up three pillows and gave them each one, keeping one for myself. I had made the flat pillows for sitting, and they weighed almost nothing. They sailed pretty well, but the impact was minimal when they hit anything.

"Let's have a pillow fight," I told them. "You can throw the pillows at each other, but they must leave your hands. You may not whack someone with your pillow."

I demonstrated, throwing a pillow that hit one of the girls in the shoulder. They giggled and got into it. Soon, we were laughing, when one of the girls looked out the window, and said, "It's snowing!" And indeed, it was.

"I don't know about you," I said to them, "but I want to go play out in the snow. Are you two ready to call it quits on the anger and go with me?"

They were delighted, and we went outside. Soon, it was recess, and I saw them walk together toward their classmates.

What started the fight? A look? A word? A gesture? They would not even know that answer themselves. I asked their teacher for more signs of this behavior, but she never referred to the incident, or the girls again. Apparently, all was well.

Word got around about my pillow fights, and one morning the vice principal, Dorothy Graham, walked in with two students. "We're at an impasse here, with a conflict, and I thought we could all benefit from a pillow fight."

I had each person pick a pillow, and I took one, too. Soon, we were tossing pillows and laughing. "Thanks," Dorothy said. "I needed that as much as they did."

I formed a sixth grade group to specifically help a large girl with the last name of "Moose." She was teased about this, and came to me in tears one day. She had finally had enough. Supported by this cluster of classmates, Sherry was encouraged to draw a cartoon of a smiling and winking moose. From then on, and with the support of her teacher, she signed all her papers with her drawing and received praise instead of ridicule.

Children who are bullied and teased by other students often need intervention from adults, but if they can devise a way to deflect this behavior in their own way, they have a tool that will help them in other situations, as well.

I invited a group of teachers to brainstorm about what worked well with disciplining students, or what created a harmonious atmosphere, and I'd like to think that they got a lot out of these sessions. I know I did. Some did tell me how they had formed small discussion groups in their classes, and how they had helped children frame requests and complaints in a more positive way.

I often visited the Kindergarten class, taught by Gloria. She played piano, and taught a lot of songs to her students. I became fascinated by these small people and their eagerness, and wondered what it would be like to teach that age.

I spent three good years at Cooper, and by the end of that time, I knew the names of nearly all the students. I learned a lot from working with these younger children, but was ready to try the skills I had learned and utilize them in my own classroom.

After three years at Cooper, I was ready to move on to a new venture.

I wanted to be a teacher again.

TEACHING KINDERGARTEN: HOW HARD CAN IT BE, ANYWAY?

During my years as counselor at Cooper Elementary, I learned to understand younger children in a school setting. I had seen how hard teachers of Kindergarten through sixth grade students worked. Compared to many of the instructors I had taught with in the higher grades, these people had to be focused and alert the entire time they presided over their classrooms. When I taught the higher grades, I could get away with easing up on a class once in a while. I would assign work to be done in class, while I sat at my desk and corrected papers. With a good, cooperative group, this was possible and even productive for the students.

Elementary teachers could not ever let their guard down. They had to be prepared for hours of lessons in all subjects, and to creatively fill the time so that their students were always busy and involved. Elementary children have shorter attention spans and a lot of physical energy, and a class can easily spin out of control.

But Kindergarten children? Why, they would be awed by this new experience, overpowered by the tall adult that reigned over them. Right?

The thought of introducing a group of children to their first public school exposure intrigued me, and I wanted to take part in this.

And here I was, the first day of class at Kimball. My bulletin boards were neatly arranged, play equipment placed strategically. A circle of flat pillows awaited the occupation of small bodies. A piece of particle board leaned against a wall, with the names of children hanging from hooks, ready for their first reading experience. A ukulele lay by a larger pillow. Several books were strewn in the middle of the circle, ready to be chosen by individuals. I would read them stories with expressive animation, and they would be awed and fascinated. They would line up nicely to go to recess. They would each have gone to the toilet before leaving home, but I would remind them, and a few would want to use our little restroom.

I was *sooo* ready.

I looked outside, through the double doors that were exclusively for my class and saw clusters of mothers and children, waiting for the bell to ring as signal for me to open the doors. Should I ask the children to line up outside, or just invite them inside and ask them to sit on pillows? I decided on the latter.

The bell rang. I opened the doors. Hanging on tight to each other, mothers and their children poured in. Parents who understood my directions asked their sons and daughters to sit down, and others followed suit. Many of the adults kissed their children goodbye and left, but some, especially Asian women who spoke little or no English, hovered around their youngsters, until I assured them that everything would be all right, and they could go. I communicated some of this with smiles and gestures and pointing. A few cried, looking back at equally anxious children, some also in tears about being abandoned by their anchors of security.

Nevertheless, my new students were soon seated, except for a few children who had wandered over to the blocks or home center, ready to play. I had to herd them back to their places and started improvising my directions by singing them to the tune of "Mary had a Little Lamb." That worked pretty well. My final song line was: "Find a pillow, everyone, and sit down on it."

Once we were all facing each other in the circle, I called out the names of a few children. Some looked confused, so I chose children that I knew would understand me: mainly African American and Caucasian students. By this time, I was standing by the particle board, pointing to the names of students I called out. The others caught on quickly, but after a half dozen names, boredom set in, and a few restless souls got up to meander around the room again. I lured them back with a song I figured they all could sing, "The Teensy Weensy Spider," and yes, most of them knew that and sang with growing confidence and enthusiasm.

I said my name, Miss Mieke, (my new principal insisted on "Miss" as part of my name) and rolled a soccer ball to an English-speaking child, Susie, asking that person to say her name and then roll it to Sam, who also understood, said his name, and passed the ball on to Gary. But then, I asked Gary to pass it to Kimi, whom I had noticed, had spoken to her mother in another language. She looked confused for a few seconds, but already having caught on to the rules, forwarded it to Jack, a Chinese boy with an American name. He also understood, and soon, everyone wanted a turn. I had passed my first test: call on English-speaking children first, and the rest will soon catch on.

I taught them a simple song with the five ukulele chords I had memorized, and ad-libbed a book with large beautiful pictures, pointing to animals and to individual children. They thought this was mighty funny, and I had to make sure that each person got to be an animal character in that book.

Gosh, they were cute. And sweet. And squirmy. And had very short attention spans. How could I entertain them for those first two and a half hours? I showed them different stations around the room, and called on each child to choose a center. The blocks and dolls were favorites. I had crayons by easels that were lined with butcher paper. I had not put out poster paints on the first day. Wise decision. Other games on display would have to be taught before anyone would be attracted to using them. I milled around, encouraging, learning their names, trying to be everywhere at once.

Survival for any elementary teacher is to know the name of each child by the time the session is over, and I was able to do that before recess.

Recess. That would be fun. I had at the ready, balls, jump ropes, and stuffed animals. We were fortunate to have our own little playground – half concrete and half grass – so we did not have to contend with older students.

"OK. Line up in two rows, everybody."

Huh?

I walked to the door and invited them to follow me. They clustered around. "I want two lines," I said again. A few pre-school veterans understood, and started forming a pair of reasonable lines. Soon, the others followed, more or less. Nothing was uniform about those lines, however. I realized this was a skill that had to be taught. It did not come naturally. I remembered Cooper School, where teachers did have two lines – one for girls and one for boys – and they would often say, "The boys lined up faster than the girls today," or some such remark.

I had decided, even then, that I would never do boys' and girls' lines. But I had to admit it was a lot easier than any other system, and I realized I had to invent more creative combinations for lining up.

Including recess, I had worked through my curriculum for the morning session in an hour and a half. What to do with the last hour? I repeated some of what I had done before. We had another play time. Another time with names. A new book. A few songs.

The bell – the blessed bell! I had an hour for lunch and setting up the room for the afternoon class.

I felt panicky. Could I actually make it through the entire day? Why hadn't it gone as smoothly as I had anticipated? Was I really cut out to teach these little people? What if I just got into my car and drove home?

Then I remembered that phrase, "Hey, Teach!" I smiled and got to work prepping for the afternoon crowd.

I would make a few changes: Ask the "animals" in the story to make sounds. Tell children to choose between being a dog or a cat. Line them up by dogs and cats. That should go well. Noisy, probably, but well. I was becoming an expert.

Wasn't I?

I was exhausted after that day of two classes. I went home and made more games. Planned more songs. Worked on fun, engaging ways to learn names, new sounds, new music. But the order I had so taken for granted, wasn't that "orderly" those first few weeks. I realized that everything had to be spelled out, guided, explained.

I was also not used to what I called the "gawkers," visitors who often walked past my area. We were considered a model school, and we all got used to being observed. However, for me, it was more of a problem, because people would stand at the edge of my classroom and say to each other, "Oh, aren't they cute? Do you see at that little boy over there with the big brown eyes? Look at how tiny that little Oriental girl is."

I tried to tell people, as tactfully as possible, that a class was in session, and would they please keep their voices down. Some even walked up to my students during the more unstructured times, and that was completely unacceptable.

I asked Phil, the principal, to talk to the visitors, so that they would leave my students alone. He understood, and the problem went away for the most part.

That first month, I lived, slept, breathed prepping for those five-year-olds. I came early, stayed hours after school, and brought work home, making games and learning materials, finding rhyme and songs, and looking for stories, finally crawling into bed close to midnight.

On a Friday evening toward the end of September, one of my colleagues and her husband invited the faculty to a party at their home. We were to bring our own steaks or lamb or pork chops to put on the barbeque, and another potluck item plus a drink of our choice. I enjoyed my meal, drank a glass of wine, and curled up in an easy chair in their living room. I learned later that people tiptoed around me, smiling. I never noticed.

I was fast asleep.

KIMBALL ELEMENTARY SCHOOL

Kimball, one of three buildings on Beacon Hill that had been built a few years before, had an "open concept" design. Teachers managed several classes in large spaces with few walls. Phil, the principal of this new venture, had chosen his staff carefully, and they had worked together for several years, housed in portables on the playground while the new school was being built, then moving into the new facility. The only person not happy with the move was the Kindergarten teacher, so the timing for Phil and me to meet was perfect. After our interview, he decided he wanted me to join the faculty, and I eagerly accepted.

The week before school started in that fall of 1973, the staff met several times, and each team carefully planned their curriculum and the methods they would use to teach blended classes – 5th and 6th graders together: about 100 children in one area, the same with 3rd and 4th graders and 1st and 2nd grade students. My space was separate, behind the office, but open to the walk-way between office and the other class areas. In the center of the school, the library served as the hub of activity, accessed easily by students from all classes.

At Kimball, our students were about 45% Asian, 35% black, and 20% Caucasian. The Chinese children, often the first generation born in this country, spoke Mandarin or Cantonese at home. The Filipinos generally had US military fathers and much younger Filipino mothers, who often taught their children Togalog or Illicano. Japanese families who had lived in Seattle for several generations were generally more affluent than the others. Their children spoke English as their main language. As the years went on, we also enrolled Vietnamese, Korean, Cambodian, and Samoan students. Most of the students, Caucasians and blacks included, were from nuclear families with a father and a mother. That changed during the nine years that I taught at Kimball.

I had worked hard that summer to prepare for my new venture. I met with Kindergarten teachers recommended to me as mentors. I visited Montessori classrooms and observed how children used the materials. I had never worked with children so young, or had any formal education in teaching five-year-olds. I hoped I wasn't in over my head.

My class area was pleasant and made for small children. The space contained two identical toilet rooms with sinks and skylights. A small wide hallway led to our own outside entrance, and children congregated in a playground built for them, with a concrete area for running and active play, and a grassy space for circle games or, on warm days, sitting with books or toys. I had inherited beautiful blocks and plastic climbing equipment, and plenty of space for the children to play and create.

BACK TO THE BASICS – WAY BACK!

For many Kindergartners, this was their first experience in a school setting. Some had been to pre-school, and those children settled down, following directions without seeming to be overwhelmed. But for others, home and parents, sometimes just one parent, was all they knew about what to expect from an adult. Many had no clue that this experience was not a one-time incident in their lives. By the second day, they started to realize it, and by the time a weekend had passed and they returned on Monday morning, they knew that this was the way much of their near-future lives would be spent.

It became a time to question the new environment: *What do I have to do to get this adult person to like me? What can I get away with? Am I safe here? Am I going to like, and be liked, by the other children? What if I can't do what the teacher wants me to do? I feel homesick. Where is mama?*

The second and third day, and the following week of that first year, were nerve-wracking for me. Several children started to assert themselves, defying my requests and bothering their classmates with poking or punching. Some cried, wanting to leave and go to the safety of their own homes and neighborhoods. I wanted to cry, too. Didn't, of course!

The most immediate problem to be addressed became apparent when at the end of that first day, several of the flat pillows I had arranged in a circle, were wet. I did not notice this until the end of the afternoon class. I simply had not paid attention. After all, we had a boys' bathroom with two stalls and a girls' room with two stalls right at the edge of the classroom, so the children could go any time they liked. Right? Well, probably in the world of older children.

I took the pillows home and washed them. As soon as the children entered the next day, I asked if anyone needed to go to the toilet. Some said "me, me!" while others raised their hands, something they had learned I pre-school, no doubt. I chose two boys and two girls and sent them to their own little rooms. Then realized I should have sent just one child at a time. How could I control the rest of the class and monitor the other four? Most wanted to try this novel activity, whether they needed to "go" or not. Would I have to specify who went where? Apparently. The boys' room had no urinals, so the two rooms were identical. I soon learned to send just one student at a time, being aware of how long that child was gone and listening for the flushing of the toilet.

Never mind getting too academic for a while, I decided. The basics were more "basic" than I had anticipated. Some children were repeat "offenders," so I called their parents and asked them to make sure their children had emptied their bladders before leaving home. I learned, through those years, that some children were simply not potty-trained by time they came to school for the first time.

Each task needed explanation. I could take nothing for granted. I soon realized that a few of the children could read at first grade level, while others had never seen a crayon or a pencil. They were worlds apart when it came to skills. We had crayon box drills, and I was grateful that the crayon boxes had just eight colors, rather than the skinnier versions of twenty-four per box.

We practiced naming the colors and taking out the correct ones as we said them. The non-English speaking kids watched the others and then began to catch on, but even some of the English-speaking children had no clue as to what crayon was what color. Some might have been partially color-blind, but I had no way of knowing this. At the end of a coloring activity, there had to be a lesson of how to put the crayons back in the boxes, one at a time.

Each activity was a learning experience, just as valid as teaching junior high students the rules of grammar or the formation of a complete sentence. I learned to appreciate each skill to be learned, like tying shoelaces and using scissors, as something valuable and to be applauded when performed well.

I settled in after a while, becoming more familiar with my charges, and they with me. The shy ones stopped being afraid. The unruly ones learned what was expected of them and settled down, more or less. Most developed tentative friendships that carried over into recess and into the choices they made with their free time. The non-English-speaking children learned enough coping behaviors with a few dozen words to make life less confusing to them. I was amazed at how fast these young brains soaked up new language skills; asking English-speaking boys and girls to follow directions first, proved to be effective. I also taught songs that would help with their vocabulary and syntax.

Toward the end of September, I was offered a student teacher from the University of Washington, and I eagerly accepted. As soon as I met Harold, I knew that this would be a blessing for both the children and for me. After all, my two groups of twenty-five very young children each were a challenge for any teacher, let alone a first-timer, like me.

I relaxed a great deal when Harold came aboard. I did not pretend to be an expert, since I had had no formal training at the elementary level of teaching, whereas that was his major.

We learned together. I decided to take charge of the morning class and use Harold as my assistant, while he ran the afternoon group, with me at his bidding. The children were delighted with the tall, laughing Mr. Browning. We were able to reach the needs of all the children, individualizing learning tasks when needed.

Harold and I played jokes on each other. One time, while he was teaching his group, I sat on the floor with the kids and interrupted by making noises and asking strange questions. He pretended to be exasperated and finally said, "Miss Mieke, either you quiet down, or you will have to leave the group and sit by yourself!" I feigned a whimper, and several children gathered around to comfort me.

Janey said, "Mr. Browning is picking on Miss Mieke!" We glanced at each other and had a tough time keeping from laughing.

When class was over, Harold said, "You just wait. I'll get you for this."

He did, but I don't remember the details, just that this time, the class was just as protective of him as they had been of me. They were, after all, magnificently compassionate little human beings, something I learned to appreciate more and more as the years progressed.

We accomplished a lot with those groups, and for the nine years I was at Kimball, I was privileged to have student teachers often. Some were more effective than others, but so much could be accomplished with an extra adult in the classroom. My favorite was Merissa, a tiny African-American woman who cast a magical spell on the students. They were eager to do almost anything for her. But she had other skills besides teaching and decided to c become a lawyer. I regretted that she would not become a teacher, because I knew how much she could have done for a generation of children.

DIVERSITY

I made generalizations about the various ethnic and racial groups in my classrooms. There were many exceptions, of course, but each year, I observed this at the beginning of the school year.

Asian children new to this country, but also of parents who had come from China, Vietnam, or South Korea and other countries, were often quiet and shy for the first few months. They had been told by their parents to "study hard and obey the teacher," and they did what was expected of them. Japanese children were generally ahead of other students, often already reading and writing.

African-American kids exuded laughter and affection, smiling and often hugging each other, me, and the adults that they knew. They added a warm and relaxed atmosphere to the classroom.

When busing became required in the Seattle district, our school received Caucasian children from several affluent areas of the city. Many of those parents had visited our school and wanted their girls and boys to have the experience of associating with children of color. These white children had gone to pre-schools and had so much parental education already, that their language skills were often more advanced. Again, the other students learned from them, as they were picking up the behaviors and attitudes of their new classmates. It was fascinating to see how these five-year-olds learned from each other.

I built diversified groups during activity times, but on the playground, the kids were on their own. This is where they sought out each other, especially the first few months: Chinese girls playing Chinese jumprope with other Chinese girls, black boys running races with each other. Later on, they meshed naturally with each other.

But those demographics happened later. For the first few years, the mix was 80% children of color.

I remember a bus trip I ordered for one of my classes, to visit Lincoln Park and look for crabs and other critters during an especially low tide. Umi came up to me in the bus and stared at me. "Miss Mieke, you are the only person on this bus with blue eyes!"

If my groups were larger than twenty-seven per class, I was allowed an aide, and my favorite was Carol. She and I worked together quite a few semesters, and again, so much more could be accomplished with the two of us.

I was privileged to share the children with many adults. When the bused-in students started to come, so did some of their mothers, who often volunteered one day a week. I would put them to work with a group or with an individual, and made sure that the group did not include their own child, so they, too, could learn from the diversity and not be in a dilemma of favoring their boy or girl. They often brought their own skills in teaching an art project, a song, or a playground game.

Yet, there were semesters where I was alone with groups of twenty-five. I always felt, even when teaching older children, that if classrooms contained no more than eighteen children, no matter what age, no special materials or programs would be needed. Forget the packaged projects that were supposed to be aids in teaching attitudes or group behavior. If a teacher wasn't into that, the kids wouldn't learn much from it anyway. ESL (English as a Second Language) might be important for older children, but at Kimball, where a half dozen of my students would be taken out for a half hour twice a week, it made little sense. I think they learned more from each other in the regular classroom than they did in that extra class. For older children, this was a good program, but at age five and six, this is simply not important.

Small classes can accommodate all but severely mentally challenged children, as well as those with mild physical handicaps, and no special classes have to set up for those with behavior problems. Unacceptable behavior can be managed by having time to praise good behavior. Those shy children that somehow slide through twelve years of not being noticed, can learn to become more assertive. Self-confident, and outstanding students can be given special projects, as well as encouragement to mentor other classmates. A teacher needs time to have a special relationship with each child, and those children are likely to flourish a lot more iif they are part of a smaller class. Unfortunately, smaller class sizes require extra rooms and a bigger staff, at a huge expense.

Books and music became the most enjoyable activity for both students and me. I read a book to them every day, adding drama to my voice and actions, asking various students to act out parts. Literature, particularly for young children, had improved greatly in the past decade, with authors such as Maurice Sendak and his most famous *Where the Wild Things Are*, Eric Carle's *The Very Hungry Caterpillar*, and Shel Silverstein's *The Giving Tree*.

Today's teachers of small children have a bonanza of literature to choose from. The publishing of beautufully illustrated books has become a cornucopia.

My students seemed to like the songs I taught them, with the aid of the few chords I had mastered on the ukulele. The

Sixties had just ended, and some of the folk music, though a bit challenging for very young voices, were their favorites. "Puff the Magic Dragon," of Peter Paul and Mary vintage, went over well, and when John Denver's "Inch by Inch, Row By Row, Gonna Make my Garden Grow" came out in the late 70's, we grabbed on to that with great gusto. But their favorite was from Cat Stevens. It was our theme song, for several years, and I remember Choi, newly arrived from Hong Kong, who would move his head from side to side in ecstasy while belting out, "Moooooon shadow moon shadow!"

THE KIMBALL STAFF

The Kimball Staff was extraordinary. The librarian, Bill made full use of the centrally located library space and his position. He "moonlighted" at Seattle University, teaching children's literature to teachers in the district. His knowledge of this subject was encyclopedic.

Anyone walking past the library would observe children from the different grades looking for books, or sitting on one of many couches, reading. Teachers brought large groups to show them how to research, or they sat on the floor while Bill entertained by reading a new book to them and telling them about the author.

At the time, the early 70's, the school had one computer, which resided in the Library. Bill was its main user and often taught small groups of older children some of the wonders of this new phenomenon. This was years before the Internet, but the computer did contain an encyclopedia, and older students were fascinated by this way of looking up information.

One of Bill's main skills was biblio-therapy, and teachers would send individual kids who might be having behavior problems, signs of depression or anger, or who knew that there was unrest in the home, to see Bill. He would spend time with each child and recommend a book that might help him or her cope with a problem. He knew enough about children's lit to talk about a character in a book who might be going through a similar situation.

The playground was overseen during recess and before school by an aide, often Carol, much beloved by the students. Five hundred students could be outside at the same time, yet fights were rare. Kids played with each other, often according to their ethnic groups. The black children, especially the boys, liked to race. Chinese girls played Chinese jump rope, with ropes they made out of rubber bands. White kids generally hung around together. There were exceptions – children from all ethnic groups doing activities with each other, like tossing footballs, shooting baskets, or playing on the monkey bars – but left to their own choosing, they mostly sought out people who looked like them, and who had similar habits and ways of speaking. We, the staff, understood this. In classrooms, we could direct our activities to mixing the different groups and having them learn from each other, but recess was their time, to be spent however they chose.

For Phil, the setting of Kimball, the demographic makeup of the students, and his hand-picked staff, "principal" was the ideal job. He had a nearly photographic memory for names, as did Bill, and would walk up to any student during an unstructured time in the classroom, in the walkways, or on the playground, and ask how things were going at home with the new baby, congratulate someone on a science project, commend a student for getting a perfect score on a spelling test, or wonder how someone had gotten a bump on the forehead.

Phil could often be seen on the playground during recess, lunchtime, or before school, where he would joke with kids and have casual conversations. If a teacher brought him two students who had started a fight or lashed out on the playground or in the classroom, he sat them down in a conference room adjacent to the office. The room had a large window, so that the two could be watched by the school secretary or by him. The culprits were told to work out the altercation between them. The phrases, "He started it," or "She did this to me" fell on deaf ears to Phil. He knew it was impossible to find out how it began: a look, a gesture, a misinterpreted grunt, even a thought about one of the kids could be the trigger, and not even those students might know what had actually started the problem.

Take away the audience of other classmates when they could show off, and those two had to deal with just each other. It usually took little time for them to come to some kind of peace, and they would be sent back to their classrooms.

One late winter, a family moved into our area: a single black mother and her five children. She enrolled them one day, and the next almost every grade level received one of her children, including mine. The newcomers were wary and shy that first day, often true of new students, but the next, chaos erupted on the playground before school and throughout the day. The new kids were picking fights, using foul language, and yelling at teachers. This behavior, so foreign to us, caught us off guard. Phil was involved all day trying to break up problems, and he decided that this would not do, even for another day.

That afternoon, after school was dismissed, he drove to Mc Donald's, filled up his car with hamburgers, milkshakes, and fries, and drove to the house. There, he fed everyone, joked with the children, asked each what they liked the most to do, and what they missed about Los Angeles. He made friends with the mother. He stayed for most of the evening, and the children were allowed to be up way past their bedtime. I would not be surprised if he might have helped tuck the younger children into bed.

That was the end of the problem. Each of those children were now Phil's friends, and for the next few days, teachers reported the good things these students were doing, so he could seek them out and commend them for their work and their behavior.

The success of a well-run school often depends, in part, on the school secretary. Evelyn was unflappable. Equally courteous and pleasant to everyone, a first grader received the same attention and care as a visitor, parent, teacher, or district administrator. Since the school nurse was not always present, Evelyn kept band-aids and other first aid equipment in a desk drawer and ice packs in the staff room refrigerator. She treated minor scrapes and bruises with care and skill where needed, and was sympathetic when any of us had real problems. But she wasn't a door mat. If any teacher came to her just before class with a test or document that she wanted mimeographed for her class, Evelyn told that person she should have taken more time to do this herself. Once, I worked in a school where the secretary had a plaque on her desk: "Lack of advanced planning on your part does not create an emergency on my part." This seemed to be Evelyn's philosophy, as well.

Even though our student population was 80% children of color, our faculty was practically all Caucasian. That changed some during the years of my tenure, but at first, we had just one African-American teacher and one Asian teacher on the staff.

Racial unrest was becoming more prevalent in the Seattle Schools, and week-long workshops were developed for school administrators and counselors, mostly geared toward junior and senior high schools. The workshops concentrated on conflict resolution and improved racial relations. The panel of these workshops consisted of adults and students of various ethnic groups. Phil felt that he wanted our entire faculty to participate, and he wrote up a grant so that each of us could take a week to immerse ourselves in this experience. 20% of our staff at a time had substitutes, until after five weeks, we had all been through the workshop, for which we received district credits.

Even though most of us felt that we taught children of color well, I think we all came away with a realization that we still were prejudiced in many areas. I know I learned that about myself, mostly by reflecting how much easier it was for me to navigate through my world more safely than, say, a black woman of my age. The term, "white privilege," was not yet used, but as time passed, I understood its meaning more and more, thanks to that intense and often humbling experience.

I thought back to my teaching year at South High School, and how that staff might have benefited from a similar workshop.

THE WORLD OF FIVE-YEAR-OLDS

In the mid-70's, the Seattle School District initiated mandatory busing for elementary students. We would lose many of our children of color to suburban schools.

We were to exchange our minority students with children from the affluent Fauntleroy and Laurelhurst neighborhoods. Many parents wanted their sons and daughters to have the experience of interacting with those of various ethnic backgrounds. In fact, after the first year, a lottery was set up, based on a waiting list of these children.

That spring, more visitors than ever came to our school: this time, parents of prospective transfer students. Even Kindergarten children were part of this, though they only came for a half day and would be spending almost half their time on the bus. Thus, my morning classes from then on would be 50% white and 50% children of color. There would be no Kindergarten busing in the afternoon, so the demographics of those classes did not change.

My mornings, especially, became filled with volunteer parents. Besides, I often had a student teacher, and sometimes even an aide. I remember one visitor who asked me, "Who's the teacher?"

I looked around the room and spied Lisa, a tiny Chinese girl, who was teaching Brucey how to tie his shoes. This was her self-proclaimed specialty, and she was proud of it.

"Oh, today it's Lisa, I believe," I told the guest.

Lisa had come a long way since the first days in September. Her mother had clung to her tearfully, and when she left, Lisa wailed. I managed to calm her down to a mere whimper, which she kept up the rest of the afternoon. At the end of the afternoon, she flung herself into the waiting arms of her mother.

Lisa arrived the second day, still in distress, still whimpering. She kept it up the entire time, although I did what I could to make her less afraid. I noticed that she was more comfortable, but she still continued the sniffles.

When she came in on the third day, still crying, I figured she was just carrying on now, and I had had enough of it. While the children sat at tables with paper and crayons, I got on top of the table where Lisa sat, and I loomed over her. Her eyes grew big, and all the children watched me with apprehension. I looked down at the tiny thirty-pound child and said in a loud, low voice, "Shut up!"

The class grew quiet. Someone started to snicker and others followed suit. Then, wonder of wonders, Lisa giggled, and so did I. We all had a great laugh. Lisa was just fine after that.

Comments from especially Asian children who were rapidly learning English, were unintentionally funny.

I remember greeting a class after the winter holiday break, and one Korean girl asking me, "You know why I was gone such a long time?"

I wondered where this was going. After all, we had all been gone a long time.

"Why, Gracey?" I asked her.

"Because I had a bacation!"

Another time, my basement had flooded one Friday while I was at work, and by the time I got home, I sloshed through three inches of water to turn off the main tap.

I spent that weekend and the following Monday cleaning up the mess, asking for a substitute for that first day of the week. When I returned on Tuesday, one of the children said, "We heard you had a flood in your basement."

Lawrence, a Chinese child of immigrants, looked at me in wide-eyed wonder, and asked, "Did you kill it?"

One November, Tracy was brought to the class by the Phil and a distraught mother. Phil wanted to enroll the large blond-haired boy in my class, explaining that Tracy had been expelled from three schools so far that year. The mother, his sole parent, was at her wits' end about how to handle him herself, and scared about his school future. She pleaded with me with her eyes, and I told her that I would be happy to take her son. I ws apprehensive, but I wanted to ease her pain, and I knew Phil would back me up.

The first day went all right for Tracy. He was sullen, watching the other children with wary eyes. By the second day, he decided to assert himself. When Carol, my aide, called for the children to line up after recess, he refused. She was faced with a dilemma. Leave him there and bring back the rest of the class? She did not dare do that, so she essentially dragged him back to the room. He glared at her the rest of the afternoon, sitting alone and not participating.

The next day, it was my turn to be tested. The pupils sat at their tables, completing a simple writing exercise. Tracy sat slouched in his seat, arms crossed. I asked him to pick up his pencil and try to write his name. He picked up the pencil, all right, and threw it at me, then got up and kicked the foot of the boy in a nearby chair.

My mind processed all this as quickly as I could. If I did not act right away, a pattern would be set up between us, and he would win.

I took hold of him, sat on the floor, and dragged him down with me, setting him down with his back toward me. I wrapped my arms around his arms and chest. He struggled with surprising strength. He tried to wriggle out of my grasp.

"Let me go," he hollered.

"I will if you promise to do your work," I told him.

"No!"

"OK, Your choice."

Tracy kicked his feet. I looped my legs around his. Now, he couldn't move anything but his head, which he banged several times against my chest.

My tactic was not totally spontaneous. I had heard about it during a workshop about discipline, and that it could have positive results. Sitting there with this squirmy, belligerent child, I only hoped I was doing the right thing.

This was before so many changes were made about contact with kids. Principals were still allowed to paddle, although I knew Phil never did. Was I within my rights to treat Tracy this way?

I asked Carol to conduct the class while I remained on the floor with Tracy. It was time for recess. Tracy demanded to go.

"You can, as soon as you do your work," I said, as calmly as I could.

"No! I won't! I want to go to recess."

"Not possible," I told him.

Fortunately, a volunteer mother was present. I asked her to stay in the room. I felt I needed a witness. Fifteen minutes later, when the class returned, I was still on the floor, holding Tracy. He was not struggling any more, and I was getting tired, too.

"How about it?" I asked him.

"No! Never! I hate you!" By now, there was weariness in his voice.

I ignored his outburst, but rocked him, while he rested his head against me. The class came back, while the two of us still sat on the floor.

Whenever a child had a birthday, the mother was invited to come and bring a party, and someone had just arrived and put out paper plates with cupcakes and cups of juice.

"I wanna go to the party!" my captive demanded.

"Very well. You know what you have to do."

"OK. I'll do my work!" he said.

I let him go. He raced to his seat, picked up a crayon and drew a picture, then signed his name. I praised him, and told him that he was welcome to participate.

The party over, it was time to go home. Tracy was all smiles as he raced toward his mother. I told Phil what I had done, and I called the mother that evening, to tell her. She seemed supportive of my discipline and grateful for anything that would work for her child.

The next day, Tracy came in subdued, but cooperative. I praised him for everything he accomplished. As the rest of the week progressed, he became more comfortable and friendly.

Why had this worked so well? According to the study, a child disciplined in this manner does not feel abandoned. I had not given him the opportunity to wriggle free, and yet, he must have felt that I cared enough about him to give him this forced hug. And indeed, I did. As I held his struggling body, my heart reached out to him.

After a week, his mother told me that he was a different person at home – happier and calmer.

Tracy, I learned, was bright and conversive. His future as a student looked promising.

I cannot imagine any teacher today, shouting at a child like I did little Lisa, or holding someone in a helpless position as I did Tracy. That person would likely be fired.

OF DINASAURS, POP CORN, AND SUCH

I don't know what there is about dinosaurs that appeals so much to small children, but they love them. They know the names and can rattle off the characteristics of the ankylosaurus, stegosaurus and triceratops, a tyrannosaurus rex and a pterodactyl, leaving most of us adults wondering where this fascination comes from.

An early morning "Aha!," which I experienced from time to time, woke me up one morning during my second year of teaching Kindergarten. When I got to school that day in early December, I told the children that I had found a basket of large eggs next to the building, and that they were now sitting under my desk, but probably not visible to them. I said they were definitely larger than chicken or duck eggs, and they were still warm. What to do?

We presumed, with a small suggestion from me, that these were dinosaur eggs, and we would set up pretend-incubators as soon as possible, so that the eggs would live. Then we carefully placed the pretend eggs into the invisible incubators and set those around the room. We counted the eggs and decided there were just enough for each child to have one as his or her responsibility.

We talked about the invisible eggs each day, and they drew pictures. Some thought they heard tiny peeps from theirs, or saw slight cracks. Throughout the next month, they added to their book of drawings and told stories that my aide or I would write down for them to copy. The librarian brought us books that I would read to the children, so they learned the names of many of these ancient creatures. The books contained pictures of eggs, so that helped.

The day before the holiday vacation, we all worried about the eggs. What would happen to them? I promised to leave the motors on in the invisible incubators.

That first day in January, when we all returned, to our surprise, most of the eggs had all hatched! Some tiny creatures were crawling around, while others were still pecking their way out of the shells. The children recognized their own, and each named the animal they were now responsible for.

We discussed the food to be collected: grasses and leaves for most, but the T-Rexes were carnevores and had to have worms at first, but later, as they grew, squirrels and rats, then larger animals, and so on.

When we sat in our circle, the "babies" nestled on the laps of their new parents. They grew, and after a while, the children sat in the laps of *their* charges. On the playground, their pretend pets puzzled the older children. What was the matter with the Kindergartners? Eventually, of course, the whole school was in on the story.

We finally decided that the classroom was no longer big enough to hold the teenage dinos, so everyone figured out how they were going to take theirs home. Some mothers came with their vans to transport their children and the new pets. Others walked home, with their stegosauruses or T-Rexes on leashes. Some flew home on the backs of pterodactyls.

For several weeks, during our morning talking time, we shared stories about how the dinos were faring, until we were pretty much done with the fantasy.

I think part of the charm of the project was that at some point, the animals were eggs, and later toddlers smaller than themselves, and that they had control over these huge creatures.

Another favorite activity involved popcorn. An instrumental song, "Pop Corn," featuring a synthesizer came out in the late 60's. It lasts approximately two and a half minutes, which is about the time it takes for a batch of corn to be popped.

I placed my electric frying pan on top of butcher paper that I arranged in a large area and asked the children to sit around this in a wide circle. I added oil and waited for the pan to heat before adding the kernels of unpopped corn. Then, with the lid off, I started the song on my cassette player. A few kernels popped high into the air, to the delight of the children, and then, more and more, so that about half way through the song, the popcorn was flying in a frenzy. Then, less and less, until, when every kernel was popped, the song was over. I allowed a few children at a time to each scoop up a handful of popcorn.

Toward the end of each May, the school put on a Dance Day, and each class was invited to perform. One time, I decided to do a popcorn dance with the children. They practiced being popcorn: scrunched over at the beginning of the song, then getting up and jumping, waving their arms, anad finally, one by one, flopping to the ground, spread out.

I asked for help from parents, collecting large white shopping bags. They turned them inside out and cut holes for the heads and two arms. We also had small white bags. On the day of the dance, my class sat toward the front on the playground in their white "costumes." Bags had been tied to their hands and feet by sixth grade students, who then escorted them to the center of the dance area.

I started the song on a turn-table tethered to a long electrical cord. One child got up and started dancing, then touched other children, one by one, who then got up and danced. The rest of the school and many parents watched, and the response was gratifying. My own parents were present, tears of laughter streaming down my mother's face.

One year, a fifth grade teacher, Ann, and I decided to team up our classes. We wrote a grant to Seattle Public Schools for all of us to visit Kelsey Creek Farm, a teaching farm in Bellevue. We received $600 for the year-long project. The first month, both classes and a number of parents went by two buses, and the older students were each paired with a Kindergartner. We surveyed the farm and met the animals: ponies, chickens, pigs, lambs, and cows. The next month, a small group of paired-up children went with a mother in her van, accompanied by a school staff person, and they got to do certain activities. Each month, a new group visited, always accompanied by a staff employee: Phil, my aide, Carol, Bill, the Librarian, Ann, or myself, and the activities ranged from brushing the ponies, gathering eggs, watching the milking, carding wool, churning butter. Each group had different projects to do, depending on the season. They would return and report their experiences to our two classes, and we made a book of pictures and stories. One lucky group witnessed the birth of a litter of piglets. Another got to pet a new-born calf and watch it drink from its mother's teats. Each season had its own characteristics, so all the children had some idea of what happens on a farm in a nine-month period of time. We ended the year by all of us going one more time by bus. In this way, each student had a chance to visit the farm three times.

It was a good experience in other ways. Older children became teachers, and the younger ones looked up to their friends. Whenever we had an all-school assembly, I would sometimes see some of my young ones run to their partners on the other side of the gym to sit with them.

On each of the farm trips, there was never a behavior problem. The fifth graders took their jobs seriously as mentors, and the younger ones idolozed their partners.

I often asked older children to help out, if their teachers could spare them for a half hour or so. For one-on-one tutoring in reading, I asked my colleagues to send children who might be having a problem socially. My kids looked up to these students, and usually, the older child would go back to his or her classroom with renewed confidence. Teachers sometimes asked if one of their students, who was having a difficult time, could come to help out. I could usually find a job for that girl or boy.

READINESS, HUMOR, MATURITY

The father of a four-year-old came to me early in September one year, to tell me how brilliant his daughter was, and that she did not belong in pre-school anymore. I am against placing children with older students, and told parents this many times. Usually they listened to me and understood that, even though a child might be academically advanced, if they waited a year, she could be on much more solid ground socially for the rest of her school life.

Rachelle's parents were adamant. Girls matured faster, they knew, and she was so far ahead of other pre-schoolers, that she belonged in my classroom. They pressured Phil, and we finally allowed her into the class. She was a tiny child, and from the very first day, she appeared frightened. I did what I could to get her involved with her classmates, but they intuitively did not truly accept her as a peer. After a week, her parents complained, saying that Rachelle often came home crying. I tried what I could, even calling her pre-school teacher, who agreed that Rachelle belonged in her classroom.

We finally got the parents to see this, too, and they moved her back to her former and more familiar environment. But they never forgave me for not trying harder, and the following year, Rachelle went to another school's Kindergarten. Her father contacted me to tell me that she was doing well there, had friends, and felt confident. He relayed this with a kind of "so there" attitude. I told him I was happy for him, and especially for Rachelle. The well-being of his daughter needed to be the ultimate goal for both of us. I smiled, but in my mind, said something snarky, like: *Duh!*

One or two children can sometimes change the climate of a classroom in a negative or positive way. The Kindergarten child of one of our teachers was unhappy in her assigned school, so he transferred her to my class, where she seemed to blossom among the other children. Her classmates loved and trusted her, and she was a leader without ever having that go to her head. She was friends with the out-going kids, but she also gave shy children her time and friendship.

Five-year-old Martin was joyous and fun. His Caucasian father and African-American mother both had college degrees. Martin was another child that other kids admired and wanted to be around.

Kindergartners have their own brand of humor. They have not yet caught on to how jokes are supposed to work. They do understand the syntax that introduces a joke, and it's easy to get them to laugh. All it takes is a sentence that begins with: "What is red and rolls down the hill?" or any such structure, and they start to laugh and give answers, such as: "a red giraffe" or "a roly-poly red ball." Pure nonsense, but not to them. The rest of the class would break into gleeful laughter at the answers.

When Martin told his joke to all of us, they also laughed, but I was amazed. "Why did Humpty Dumpty have a great fall?" he asked the class. This evoked nonsense answers from the other kids, but I wondered where he was going with this.

"Why, Martin?" I asked him.

"Because he had a rotten summer."

This was truly funny. This sophistication does not show up until about second grade.

Encouraged, he told other jokes that were organized and humorous. "What do you call a scared skin diver? Chicken of the Sea." This induced laughter from the others, but they had no idea what he was talking about.

There is as much academic and social difference between Kindergarten children as there is at any other grade level. Some enter without ever having used a crayon or a pencil. Some can read at a first grade, even higher level. It is unrealistic to expect sending a class on to first grade with every individual knowing how to read simple sentences. For many, learning to get along with classmates, following directions, coloring, using scissors, pasting, drawing, even using the bathroom, are skills that need to be learned first.

Parents often told me, with pride, that their boy or girl knew how to read, when they meant that that child could recite the alphabet, or even that he or she recognized letters. But to translate that into understanding that these letters formed words that had meaning, is a more advanced skill. Some children get this without difficulty, but for others, it takes months. I often observed children who saw letters as some kind of isolated skill that they were supposed to learn to please parents and teachers. It was always exciting to me to see someone suddenly catching on to what these letters could do when organized into words and sentences. These fortunate kids soared, almost overnight, into readers.

I remember one parent observing my class in the spring, during the children's activity time. She was contemplating enrolling her daughter the following fall. "Shirley knows how to read already," she told me, in an arrogant tone. "Will that be a problem?"

I smiled back reassuringly. "Not at all," I said. "Because you know what? I know how to read, too." A bit of a sarcastic reply, I suppose, but I couldn't resist.

I found it challenging and fascinating to work with the written language on so many levels of skills. I encouraged the readers to become writers. I watched for that spark that would turn a letter-recognizer into a sounds and words reader, and finally into understanding whole sentences that made sense. Everyone learns at his or her own individual pace, no matter how much group effort is emphasized and encouraged. A teacher who gets that will encourage those who are ready, to soar while being patient with others who don't yet have that maturity.

Large classes make this difficult. Whenever I was lucky enough to have a class, no matter what grade level, of fifteen and eighteen students, I felt fortunate, both for the students and for me. So much could be accomplished.

COOPERATION AT KIMBALL

One year, a snow storm brewed an hour before the children were to leave. By the time the buses arrived, the roads were already slick. Worried parents called, and an hour after we had dismissed the kids, many were not home yet. This was long before the time of cell phones, so the office phone rang off the hook. Several teachers ventured out in their own cars to track down children not yet accounted for, and none of us left until we were satisfied that all were safely home. It was already dark, and we had to venture home as best we could to our own homes.

I saw compassion in my classes many times. A Vietnamese child, Hu Tan, newly arrived and not yet speaking much English, would finish his art project, then look around the room for someone struggling with hers, and help out until she was finished. After a coloring session, he surveyed all the crayon boxes, making sure the right colors were put back in each one.

Maryanne, from a Filipino family, was nearly a head taller than the other children and weighed 130 pounds. She spoke no language, neither English or her own native Illicano, although she knew enough to understand her parents. Her cognitive capacity had been diagnosed as that of a two-year-old. She communicated by hugs, which she did frequently with all of us. When she sat in our circle, children snuggled next to her, as if she were a soft, warm pillow. Several girls tried to teach her to speak.

Jamila lay a book on Maryanne's lap and opened it up to pictures of animals. "Maryanne, this is a sheep. Say "sheep."

Maryanne would not, because she could not. She just smiled contentedly.

One day, while walking through the building to the gym, I saw that older children were snickering and pointing. When we got back to our classroom, Peter said, with indignance, "Some big kid said, 'There goes that big fat girl!'"

The rest of the class nodded solemnly. They were not a bit amused.

I reported the incident to some of my colleagues, and they promised they would talk to their students.

Maryanne left in the middle of the school year. She had been evaluated by a doctor and psychologist and had gone through a number of tests. Apparently, she had a small, under-developed brain and was not expected to live past her tenth birthday.

Her mother told me that they could not control her at home, and that she had a temper that could flare at a moment's notice. Much had to do with food. They had to put a padlock on the refrigerator and any cupboard that contained food. She wanted to eat all the time.

She did not get that chance in the classroom, so it was not an issue. She loved our school and her classmates.

The other children missed her when she left. A few months later, I was at a meeting with her new special education teacher, who asked, "Are you the person who sent us that fat girl that wants to hug everybody all the time?"

"Well, that's how Maryanne communicates." I told him.

"We put a stop to that," he said. "And you know what she did? She stalked out of the classroom and somehow got to the parking lot, where she was snapping off antennas until we caught her."

I felt sick. I had abandoned her. Or at least, that is how it must have felt to her.

I was relieved to learn that she had been transferred to the University of Washington in a special education program for children with severe cognitive learning disabilities. The school had a great reputation and I knew they could do much more for her than I could have.

SHARING BOOKS AND FILMS WITH STUDENTS

Most parents and teachers will agree: sharing worthwhile books and movies with children is one of the best activities spent together. It affords the opportunity to talk about the stories and to teach students the value of understanding the viewpoint of characters and the writers who create them. I am not now, and was not when I was teaching, encyclopedic about children's literature. I admire people who are, and often consulted school librarians and other teachers for the right gem to share with a classroom or an individual student.

Now, thirty-five years after ending my teaching career, some stories stand out in my mind that touched my students, and spurred lively discussions.

When I taught high school, certain pieces of literature were required reading at each grade level. During the year I taught tenth graders, I was to expose them to Shakespeare's Julius Caesar. To the advanced class, I loaned each a booklet with a copy of the play, and with a combination of homework and in-class reading, we sailed through this smoothly, since students were intrigued with the story. The class with more learning difficulties needed a different approach. I ordered a film of the play, but when I turned it on, there was no sound. Several tech-savvy boys gave suggestions, but nothing worked.

So I decided to show the movie without sound, and the students watched with curiosity. I turned off the projector at the beginning of Mark Anthony's speech. I told the class the entire story they had seen, through the speech in which Brutus convinces the crowd that assassinating Caesar had been the right, moral, and patriotic move, and he had made himself out to be a hero for risking his own life to kill the Emperor. Then, I told them that Mark Anthony got up to address the crowd, and, in one powerful speech, he completely turned around the audience into believing that Caesar had been a noble leader, and Brutus, a traitor.

That's all I told them; a number of my students were curious enough to check out booklets and read the rest of the play on their own. The next day, I showed another version of Julius Caesar, this time with sound, and by the time we talked about it, most of the class seemed to understand and appreciate the essence of the story.

I shared one of my favorite all-time books with my seventh-grade classes:*The Greatest Thing Since Sliced Bread,* by Don Robertson, reporter for Cleveland's *The Plain Dealer,* published in 1965. Nine-year-old Morris Bird the Third decides to go on a quest to find his friend, who has moved to the other side of Cleveland. He takes his Crimson Streak wagon and his little sister, who threatens to tell if he doesn't let her come along, and they launch out, getting caught in the historic Cleveland fire. The writing is beautiful and sensitive, showing the courage of this unpretentious child. It generated discussions of heroism and loyalty. The little novel reminds me of Ray Bradbury's *Dandelion Wine* for its style and *To Kill A Mockingbird* for the nobility of children.

To Kill a Mockingbird came out in the late 60's as well, and that was perfect for reading and discussion with 9th graders. It provoked an examination of racial tension, particularly in a small town, and how this created a bond between a father and his daughter. It was also a book about children and for children that featured a girl as the main protagonist, relatively rare at that time. Again, the writing is superb, and it was great for reading aloud to my classes.

I taught Kindergarten through the 70's, and books and films for small children were becoming more available

Two balloon stories stand out in my mind. Most people have seen the famous French film, *The Red Balloon*, about a boy who is taunted by older children, who are trying to take his balloon, but because of his courage, all helium balloons owned by children are released and float toward him, until they lift him up and fly him over the city of Paris.

A lesser-known movie and book called *The Blue Balloon*, features a little boy in a New York tenement house, who is given a blue balloon, and he is entrnaced by this magic. He hangs onto the string and floats it out the window, where the sun shines through it. But then he lets go of the string, and it soars away, out of sight. He is heartbroken and starts to cry. He cries and cries. His parents are concerned, but they understand, and they let him cry. He goes to his room and cries some more, while his family eats dinner. But then the crying stops, and he comes to the dinner table.

"Are you all right?" his mother asks.

"Yes," he answers, sitting down. "I'm through."

The five-year-olds were touched by the story, and by the conclusion. They understood why the mourning period was over, at least enough so that the boy could pursue his normal activities again. Would he forget his balloon? No, they decided. But it was now a memory.

My favorite movie to show Kindergartners was *The Tree House*. An eight-year-old boy has a house in an old gnarled oak tree. He loves to climb up to spend time with his comic books, his binoculars, and a snack that his mother has prepared for him.

Daily, he watches, far in the distance, as a John Deere Caterpillar takes down trees and other vegetation. He is pleased that now he can see much farther, all the way to the river. Every day, the large yellow vehicle comes closer, clearing more land, until he can see the man in the driver's seat; the man sees him, too, and smiles at him…

One day, the man is not smiling. He tells the boy, "You need to come down from the tree. It's – it's – time to come out of the tree."

"Why?" asks the boy, puzzled and alarmed.

"It's coming down. The tree is coming down," says the man in a hoarse voice.

Realization dawns in the boy. He tenses and his face takes on a defiant look; he crosses his arms and stares at the man. The man coaxes him some more, until the boy throws his treasures to the ground and stomps down out of the tree, in tears.

Too traumatic for five-year-olds? Some cried, but we could talk about it, and they identified with the boy. Not all stories have happy endings, as was often true in their own lives.

I would like to have shown this to 10th graders. The movie had been filmed in the early 60's, when tract housing was prominent. Tear down every piece of vegetation to build houses "made of ticky-tacky." It would have touched the older students in yet another way.

With the younger children, I would hold up the books to show pictures and dramatize the reading. This comes naturally to all of us when we read to children. The older students sat at their desks, some with rapt attention on their faces, some slouched in their seats, some doodling with pen or pencil on paper, some with heads down on their desks, sleeping, or just listening with their eyes closed. It was hard to tell how engaged each student was, but most enjoyed those reading hours. I hoped it would encourage them to read on their own, as many of them already did, and to have a richer understanding of their world and compassion for those whose experiences may be different from theirs.

GROWING AS A TEACHER

I still remember that first day of my teaching life in Bremerton, when Miss Crawford invited me into her classroom with the recycled bulletin board items: "Fall means a new School Year," she told me, "to be changed in 'November for Holiday Time,'" from boxes in her attic, only to be stuffed back in for the next segment, "Winter Means Snow." She had made these years ago, and saved herself a lot of time by recycling them, rather than making up a whole new display.

She had been in this classroom for twenty-five years, she told me proudly, and hoped to finish her career in this same room in fifteen. Since the school burned down five years later, she never accomplished this plan. I don't know what happened to her after that, and how she dealt with this disruption of her well-ordered, and what I judged, boring, career.

That was not my vision of my idealized teaching career. This incidental encounter did much to direct my future course. I had no long-range plan, and from that day on, that *was* my plan: take each year as its own experience.

The first year was far from perfect; in fact, every year was far from perfect. But at the end of each term, I knew that the *next* time, I would be totally organized and on top of every situation, every project, every problem child. That hope, that dream, was how I started each fall when the doors opened to my new groups of students. It never worked out exactly that way.

Reflecting back, which is now nearly forty years ago, the richest times I spent with children from age four to seventeen were the unplanned, the spontaneous, even some of the seeming failures, from which we all survived – teacher and students, and grew.

I was a good teacher, with less-than-desired results, in my estimation, but also with projects that went beyond anything I expected. In each school where I taught, I recognized great teachers, and did not put myself in that category. There was always, always, always, room for improvement.

What remained constant in my interaction with children, whether they were six or fifteen? I generally identified with each individual. If someone was sad or belligerent, I did not need to know the details, just how it *felt* to be that way, and it helped me to be patient. I took for granted that some pupils are stars in the eyes of their classmates. They are the outgoing, extroverted people who sail through life being leaders, generally feeling confident in their interaction with the world and their contemporaries.

Others are introverts, as am I, and need alone time, even in a crowded classroom. The child who doesn't pay attention but daydreams by looking out of the window instead of at the teacher, is not necessarily lazy or disrespectful. I remembered many times in my own life where I would, and still will, do that same thing.

At Kimball Elementary, the last school where I taught and the longest assignment – nine years – a practice was enacted by us, the staff, that lasted for many years, long after

I left. After recess, when the children came back into the classroom, the entire school observed twenty minutes of silence. Since the classrooms were open and flowed into each other, with carpeting everywhere, this was a hospitable climate for that time of quiet. Children sat at desks or on the floor. So did teachers. Some read, some doodled on paper, many lay down and slept. Some stared into space. Some prayed. The only rule was complete silence. We were convinced that this helped to shape an environment of peace and harmony.

My practice of reading to each class for a half hour per week in junior and senior high, and the daily sessions with Kindergartners, allowed children to absorb this experience, or even not to absorb it in their own way, without interference from me.

Through the years, I endured difficult children, and they had to put up with me. I did not get along with some students, and would spend the rest of the year feeling as though I had failed that boy or that girl. Sometimes it was because our personalities just plain clashed.

I remember a ninth grade girl who wanted to learn the basics of grammar and diagraming, and I did not emphasize that in the way that Mr. Leonard did. Her parents came to see me about the dilemma. I invited Betsy to sit in on the conference. Was there some way I could adjust my teaching? I suggested that, since the girl felt she would be happier in Mr. Leonard's class, why not make that switch? No, her parents wanted her to be able to learn to deal with people she did not get along with. I convinced them that what was best for Betsy was to put her in the classroom where she felt she could learn the most.

They finally agreed, and I noticed, in the following weeks whenever I saw Betsy in the halls, that she was a much happier person. I asked her how she liked her new classroom and teacher, and she told me that she was doing well. I would like to think she appreciated my intervention.

Often, seeing the humor in a strange situation was a saving grace, for students and for me. I remember one seventh-grade girl coming to class one day, giggling, and followed by friends who were also snickering. What was going on? I wondered. It was tough to get the class to settle down, and I was the only one in the room, apparently, who was not in on the joke, whatever it was.

About half way through the 50-minute session, Linda popped out of her seat and said to me in a half-whispered, panicky voice, "I gotta go to the bathroom!" and ran out of the room. With some concern, I worried about the urgency, but went on with the class. When she did not return within a reasonable amount of time, I sent another girl to check on her. That student came back and told me, "She needs to see you."

I hated to leave my class, but saw no recourse but to ask the others to do work on something while I was gone. In the restroom, Linda was standing by a sink, in tears, holding up her dripping purse. "I told the kids I had a bottle of beer in my purse, but it's root beer. My dad makes it, but I guess it exploded in my purse!"

I took in the situation: her earlier braggadocio that had led to a lot of attention from her classmates, and the melt-down unfolding in front of me.

"I'm sorry! I'm sorry!" she said. "You're going to send me to the principal."

I looked at her and the soggy mess she was holding. I put an arm around her and suppressed the urge to laugh. "Well," I told her, chuckling, "you ruined your purse. That's enough trauma for one day. I'll send someone in to help you clean up the mess. I have a paper bag in my desk, and you can put everything in that. Just make sure you dry things off so the bag won't break."

Linda smiled and let out a sigh of relief. She did not need a lecture, or punishment. She already knew she had brought this on herself, and in a week or so, she would be able to laugh at the memory of this dilemma.

During my teaching years, I learned that children often learn behavior by trial and error, and also by example. Admonishing someone is often not necessary. An action, and its consequence, is generally the best teacher. I often found it helpful to ask a person, "What do you think you could have done differently?" Most kids can figure this out, and it helps to allow them to verbalize it. This empowers them to learn to trust their own wisdom.

WRAP-UP OF MY TEACHING CAREER

I spent twenty-one years of my early adult life teaching students between the ages of four and eighteen. For two of those years, I lived in Frankfurt, Germany, teaching American children of Army parents. For one year, I taught in Grand Rapids, Michigan, and the rest of the time, in Washington State, starting my career in Bremerton and ending in Seattle.

My yearly classes averaged about twenty-five students: sometimes two groups per day, spanning three sessions each: some, three groups in two-hour blocks, other times, five classes each day, with a change each semester. During the three years that I was an elementary counselor, I got to know most of the 500 or so students, so the total number of students I got to know was approximately 1800.

For us teachers, that's a lot of names to learn. Most of us waste no time learning those names. By day two or three, I had that pretty well mastered. With Kindergarten kids, I learned the names of the parents, too, since many showed up often to bring and pick up their children or to help in the classroom.

Every year, I vowed to be the perfect teacher, having learned from all the mistakes of past years. Some years were better than others. Some were so rewarding that I wondered why I was being paid for this job in the first place. In other years, I felt I wasn't paid nearly enough.

Some strategies I learned at the time wouldn't work well today, since conditions are so different. I would not want to teach now, with all the expectations and restrictions put on teachers. And today's students are facing much more serious social problems, both at home and with their peers, than what I had to contend with some forty years ago. But at the time, I learned what I needed to understand the children of the sixties and seventies.

I took classes on discipline and behavior, but most of it I learned on my own, through trial and error, and my own sense of knowing what was fair, what students would respond to, what would help them to excel in what they aspired to become.

I learned that junior high students had their own brand of humor, transitioning from innocent and corny to slightly bawdy, to outright unacceptable, and I walked that fine line with them often, since I did not want to squelch a humorous comment if it was within my bounds of what I deemed appropriate.

The year I taught at Wilson, I invited my students to decorate one of the bulletin boards by cutting pictures out of magazines and finding phrases to "explain" the illustrations. The results were clever and funny, and students from other classes would wander in during break times to laugh or offer suggestions. The principal even checked it out from time to time, because some of the contributions bordered on risqué. I reserved the right to edit accordingly, of course.

Adolescent kids are growing fast and getting used to new height, new strength, and hormones invading their bodies at a rapid rate. And they are loveable or annoying, depending on a teacher's own tolerance for the unexpected.

Around ninth grade, students settle down a bit, and by tenth, there is a new confidence now that their bodies are adult, that they can quit school if they want to, that they can drive, that they are often left home alone, and expected to be responsible.

Eleventh graders are more serious. By this time, they have decided that they will stay in school and graduate, so studying becomes more important. They are thinking college and jobs, and many already have part-time employment.

I never taught a class of seniors, but did have a senior home room. Many of them would often not show up, and it was hard to know if this was because of a job, or some kind of office they held in a student organization, or if they were just skipping that day. They would, however, attend the classes taught by really good teachers, or if they needed that particular course to help them launch their college career.

Many senior-year students were applying to colleges and universities, and signing up for interviews with personnel from various institutions.

As a counselor, I learned that, in general, elementary teachers are more dedicated and serious about their teaching than some who teach junior and senior high. They have to be. They cannot leave their classrooms, or be busy at their desks while the students do work on their own.

I ended my career by teaching five-year-olds, who need the most constant care of all students. It was rewarding, if often exhausting work.

What level did I enjoy the most? What I liked about both Kindergartners and seventh graders was their orientation into a new phase of their lives, and being a facilitator for that. I liked eighth graders for the very thing many teachers found annoying: their unpredictable behavior and whacky sense of humor. I loved the challenge of getting them to like and trust me.

Discussions with 10th and 11th grade students were often challenging and fun, but that could happen in junior high, as well. Not possible with five-year-olds, except at a very basic level. To be fair to them, they often said some very profound things.

After those twenty-one years, I felt it was time to move onto a different phase of my life, one in which I would have more time to write. I always saw teaching as an important part of my life, but not a life-long career.

My heart goes out to those who do remain in this profession, often making life-long differences in the lives of their students. I'm sure this is still true today, but it is a lot harder, with so many restrictions, and a host of mentors, both beneficial and detrimental, readily available on social media today.

POSTSCRIPT

Many incidents of my teaching career stand out in my memory, but few more fondly than this, in one of my last years of teaching Kindergartners:

Travis loved to run. Whenever the children went to the playground, he joined a group of boys that ran from the wall of the building to a patch of grass some eighty feet in the distance, where they would collapse and roll over, before getting up and running back. After the winter break that year, he showed off his new tennis shoes. He told me, "I can run so fast in my new shoes, that Grandpa told me that I'm going to be an Oh-lympic star someday, like Jesse Owens!"

During their daily sprints he arrived first on the grass almost every time, in spite of his short stature.

A few months later, a new student arrived. Noah, tall, sunbleached hair, tanned by the Hawaiian sun, watched the runners during that first recess, then joined them, sailing past them with speed and agility way beyond his years.

I watched my little friend, as he took it in. "Poor Travis," I thought, until he came trotting toward me, his eyes aglow with excitement.

"Miss Mieke, did you see that new boy, Noah? He runs so fast, he's gonna be an Oh-lympic star some day!"

Moved nearly to tears, I hunkered down and took hold of his hands. "He's pretty good, isn't he? But so are you. You and Noah will be running friends, I can tell."

To myself, I said, "Someday, Travis, when I grow up, I want to be just like you."

During the nine years that I was privileged to be a Kindergarten teacher, those five-year-olds taught me much about compassion, generosity, spontaneity, fun, and energy.

I grew up and learned to be more like them.